# THE GIFT OF WISDOM
## The Books of Prophets and Writings

Steven E. Steinbock
**Illustrated by Ahuva Mantell**

**Dr. S. David Sperling, Consulting Editor**

**UAHC Press**
New York, New York

This book is dedicated to teachers, and in particular, to those who provided the mortar that shaped this book. Bonia Shur, Joel L. Levine, William Cutter, and Howard I. Bogot.

*The stone that the builders rejected has become a cornerstone.*

PSALM 118:22

Library of Congress Cataloging-in-Publication Data

Steinbock, Steven E.
The gift of wisdom: the books of Prophets and Writings / Steven Steinbock;
illustrated by Ahuva Mantell; S. David Sperling, consulting editor.
p.   cm.
ISBN 0-8074-0752-6 (pbk.: alk. paper)
1. Bible. O.T. Prophets (Nevi'im)—Juvenile literature. 2. Bible. O.T.
Hagiographa—Juvenile literature. [1. Bible. O.T.—Study and teaching.] I. Mantell,
Ahuva, ill. II. Sperling, S. david. III. Title.

BS1286 .S74 2001
221.6'1—dc21

00-068271

Design by Itzhack Shelomi

# Contents

# Acknowledgments

I am grateful to Rabbi Hara Person for her patience and dedication in editing this book, and Dr. S. David Sperling for his conscientious and probing analysis of the text. I would also like to thank all those at the UAHC who worked so hard on this book: Debra Hirsch Corman, Liane Broido, Ken Gesser, Stuart Benick and Rick Abrams. I was assisted by a number of young readers who reviewed my work at various stages: Petra Lehman, John Bartholomew, and Myles Lazar. I owe much to my parents, Richard Steinbock z'l and Jo Ann Steinbock z'l, as well as my wife, Sue, and two sons, Nathaniel and Samuel, for giving me the space and support to complete it.

# Chapter One

## THE WORLD OF PROPHETS AND WRITINGS

*In this chapter, we will take our first look at the eight books that make up N'vi-im* נְבִיאִים, *the prophetic books of the Bible. As we learn how these books are a part of the Bible as a whole, we will begin to understand who the prophets were, when they lived, and what they did.*

The Bible is a huge book. Young people and grown-ups alike can be discouraged by a book so long and with so many different kinds of writings. The word "Bible" comes from the Greek word for "books."

*The Bible is a collection of many books!*

Scholars disagree about how many books there are in the Bible. Some count thirty-nine books. Others say that the total is twenty-four.

To make things a little simpler for us, we divide the Jewish Bible into three groups of books. Think of them as three shelves.

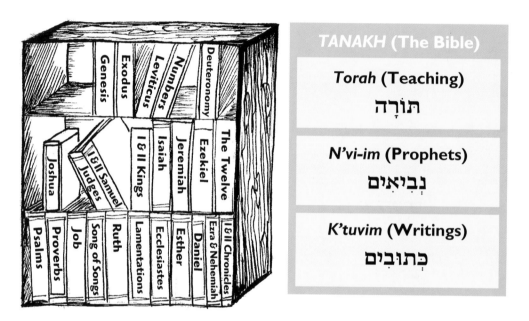

*Tanakh* is one of the names we use for the Bible. The word *Tanakh* is an abbreviation made up of the names of the three groups of books in the Jewish Bible: *Torah* תּוֹרָה—*N'vi-im* נְבִיאִים—*K'tuvim* כְּתוּבִים.

In this book, we will be learning about the eight books that make up *N'vi-im* נְבִיאִים, as well as the eleven books that comprise *K'tuvim* כְּתוּבִים.

We will learn about the judges, prophets, and kings of Israel. In this survey of the books of the Bible, we will cover one thousand years of Jewish history, from the arrival of the Israelites in Canaan until the time of the Maccabees. We will explore the many beliefs and ideas of our ancestors that shaped what Judaism is today.

You have probably learned about Torah in past years. The Torah is made up of five books that tell the stories of the early days of civilization and of the people Israel, who later became known as the Jewish people. In it are stories of Adam and Eve, Noah and the Flood, Abraham and Sarah, Jacob and Rebekah, and Joseph in Egypt. The last four books of the Torah tell how Moses led the Israelites out of Egypt and through the desert, where they received the Torah and became a unified people.

This collection of five books is called *Torah* תּוֹרָה—or "Teaching"—because our tradition teaches that God gave these books to Moses as a set of instructions to teach to the Jewish people. These instructions told the people how to live a holy life: celebrating holidays, preparing offerings to God, caring for the poor and needy, taking care of the land, and getting along with each other.

# *N'vi-im*: The Prophetic Books of the Bible

| The Eight Books of *N'vi-im* | |
|---|---|
| Joshua | יְהוֹשֻׁעַ |
| Judges | שׁוֹפְטִים |
| Samuel | שְׁמוּאֵל |
| Kings | מְלָכִים |
| Isaiah | יְשַׁעְיָהוּ |
| Jeremiah | יִרְמְיָהוּ |
| Ezekiel | יְחֶזְקֵאל |
| The Twelve | |

When you see the word "Prophets" in this book, it can have one of two different meanings:

The Prophets are a set of eight books in the *Tanakh*.
The prophets were men and women who spoke for God.

Names can be confusing. Joshua is the name of a person as well as a book in the *Tanakh*. To distinguish the names of books in the *Tanakh* from the names of people, book names will appear in **bold type** in this textbook.

We don't always know who wrote the books in the *Tanakh*. Of the many books that are named for people (**Joshua**, **Samuel**, **Isaiah**, **Jonah**), some may have been written by the person for whom they were named. A prophet named Ezekiel, for instance, probably wrote much of the Book of **Ezekiel.**

The word "prophetic" means "of the prophets," so we sometimes call *N'vi-im* "the prophetic books."

There are eight books in the Prophets section of the *Tanakh*. The first four books—**Joshua, Judges, Samuel,** and **Kings**—are sometimes called the "Historical Prophets." These books tell us about the history of the Israelite nation after its return from Egypt.

The next four books are sometimes called the "Literary Prophets." These books—**Isaiah, Jeremiah, Ezekiel,** and **The Twelve**—contain speeches, poems, and stories written by various prophets in ancient Israel.

---

### DID YOU KNOW...?

Two of the books in Prophets, **Samuel** and **Kings**, are so long that most Bibles separate them into four different books: **First Samuel, Second Samuel, First Kings,** and **Second Kings.**

The Book of **The Twelve** is sometimes called the "Minor Prophets" and sometimes the "Later Prophets." These are actually twelve different books that are so short, the ancient Rabbis grouped them together as one. They include:

| | | | | | |
|---|---|---|---|---|---|
| 1. Hosea | הוֹשֵׁעַ | 5. Jonah | יוֹנָה | 9. Zephaniah | צְפַנְיָה |
| 2. Joel | יוֹאֵל | 6. Micah | מִיכָה | 10. Haggai | חַגַּי |
| 3. Amos | עָמוֹס | 7. Nahum | נַחוּם | 11. Zechariah | זְכַרְיָה |
| 4. Obadiah | עוֹבַדְיָה | 8. Habakkuk | חֲבַקּוּק | 12. Malachi | מַלְאָכִי |

---

How does God speak to us? In the Torah, God spoke to our ancestors through dreams, messengers, or visitors. The Hebrew word for angel—*malach*—means nothing more than "messenger." God spoke through miracles such as a burning bush and a pillar of smoke and fire. For the prophets, God spoke through beautiful images and through the "still, small voice" of conscience.

# What Is a Prophet?

The English word "prophet" comes from a Greek word meaning "one who speaks before"—before something happens—in other words, someone who predicts the future. The Hebrew word *N'vi-im* means "people called [by God]."

People today often use the word "prophet" to mean someone who can guess the future.

**Anyone** can guess the future. And in fact, many of the prophets wrote about visions they had of future events.

Predicting the future was not as important to the prophets of the Bible as telling the people to listen to God. Sometimes the prophets would tell what **might** happen. Good things would come, they said, if we walked the path of God. Bad things would happen if we turned away from God. Predicting the future was not the most important thing that the prophets did.

The "job" of a prophet was to speak for God. The prophets shared God's words with the people through poetry and speeches.

On the following page are some passages from the Torah that describe prophets. Read the passages carefully. Each one tells something about what a prophet does. In the space provided, complete the sentence "A prophet is a person who…" according to the passage.

| TORAH PASSAGE | WHAT DOES EACH PASSAGE TELL US ABOUT PROPHETS? |
|---|---|
| Two men, one named Eldad and the other Medad, stayed at camp. And the Spirit rested upon them…and they prophesied. A boy told Moses that Eldad and Medad were running around acting like prophets.…Moses said, "If only all God's people were prophets with God's spirit on them." <br> NUMBERS 11:26–29 | A prophet is a person who… |
| God said: "When a prophet of God arises among you, I will make Myself known to him in a vision; I will speak to her in a dream." <br> NUMBERS 12:6 | A prophet is a person who… |
| [God told Moses]: "I will raise up a new prophet, like yourself, from among [the Israelites]. I will put My words in his mouth and he will tell [the Israelites] all that I command him." <br> DEUTERONOMY 18:18 | A prophet is a person who… |
| Balaam said to Balak: "Do I have the power to speak freely? I can say only the words that God puts in my mouth." <br> NUMBERS 22:38 | A prophet is a person who… |

The job of a prophet was not a simple one. As we read and discuss texts from *Tanakh*, your understanding of prophets will grow.

Think of a prophet as…

A newspaper columnist who writes editorials that challenge governments and businesses to behave differently.

A football coach who yells at his team when they aren't working hard enough, but who comforts them when they lose.

A poet or folksinger who writes songs that are sometimes sweet, sometimes bitter, sometimes soothing, and sometimes angry.

# Prophets in Torah

If you've learned about the Torah, you can probably already name several prophets. Below are some of the prophets found in the Five Books of the Torah. See if you can match them with their descriptions.

**Aaron**          The greatest prophet of Israel told God he didn't want to be a prophet, because he was "slow of tongue."

**Balaam**         God told Moses to take this person, his brother, as a prophet.

**Miriam**         God promised this prophet that he would be the father of a great nation, and that is what his name means.

**Abraham**        This prophet used music and dance to communicate with God.

**Moses**          This non-Israelite prophet was hired by a wicked king to curse Israel, but only blessings could come out of his mouth.

# Moses: No Greater Prophet

The Torah ends with the death of Moses. This is how the Torah describes our greatest teacher:

Never again was there a prophet like Moses in all of Israel. God *chose* him, *face-to-face,* for the various *miracles and warnings* that God had him show to the land of Egypt, and for all the *strength and power* that Moses had leading Israel.

DEUTERONOMY 34:10–12

Complete the following sentences with phrases from the above text.

God _____ Moses, _____.

Moses showed the Egyptians _____.

Moses showed the Israelites _____.

What do the words of that text, from the last verses of Deuteronomy, teach us about what a prophet is and what a prophet does?

_____

_____

_____

# What about *K'tuvim?*

In the later chapters of this textbook, you will be reading from and learning about the books of *K'tuvim*. *K'tuvim* means "Writings." There are eleven books in *K'tuvim*. (There are thirteen if we count **First** and **Second Chronicles** as two books and **Ezra** and **Nehemiah** as separate books. Traditional Hebrew texts of the *Tanakh* count these as two rather than four books.)

What kind of writings do we find in *K'tuvim?* Just about everything under the sun!

- There are books of poetry, such as **Psalms, Lamentations,** and **Song of Songs.**

- There are books of ideas, teachings, and philosophies, which include **Proverbs, Ecclesiastes,** and **Job.**

- There are stories and historical books, like **Ruth, Daniel,** and **Ezra/Nehemiah.**

The books of *N'vi-im* and *K'tuvim* were written over a long period—almost a thousand years. Generally, the prophetic books were written before 459 B.C.E., while the Writings were written over a long period between the ninth and second centuries B.C.E.

Just as the books of the *Tanakh* follow, more or less, a historical order, as you read *The Gift of Wisdom* you will be learning about these books, more or less, in the order they were written.

*In this chapter, you were introduced to the Prophets and Writings sections of the Bible. There are eight books of* N'vi-im, *which contain stories, history, poems, and lessons for the ancient Israelite nation. The eleven books of* K'tuvim *include books of poetry, philosophy, stories, and history. As we read these texts from the Prophets and Writings, we will find that they have lessons for us, as they have for Jews and Christians for thousands of years.*

# Chapter Two

## JOSHUA: A NEW LEADER FOR ISRAEL

*We now take a close look at the first chapter of* **Joshua**. *This text is the first section of* N'vi-im. *It continues from the point that the Torah ended. Moses has just died, and Joshua—the new leader of the people of Israel—is bringing Israel into Canaan, the "Promised Land."*

In the last chapter, we learned that Moses was the greatest teacher—and greatest prophet—that Israel ever had. It is sad that Moses worked so hard to bring the Israelites into the land of Canaan but was never able to enter that land himself.

Imagine that you are a news reporter, covering the story of Israel entering the Promised Land. You have the opportunity to interview God and Moses. How would they answer your questions?

| "God, why didn't you let your servant Moses have a chance to enter the land promised to Israel?" | "Moses, can you comment on your reaction to God's announcement that you will die before you ever see the Promised Land?" |
|---|---|
| | |

At the end of **Deuteronomy,** the fifth book of the Torah, Moses died. Nobody was there to bury him. He died—alone with God—at an unnamed spot east of the Jordan River overlooking the Judean Hills. The text tells us that he was buried by God.

Now a new leader was needed to stand before God and the people Israel.

That person was Joshua, son of Nun. Joshua served Moses, first by investigating the land and people of Canaan, and then by being Moses' assistant.

Joshua would be a good leader for Israel. Moses admired him because he was honest, realistic, and a good military man.

The Book of **Joshua** is the first book of the *N'vi-im* נְבִיאִים—the Prophets—section of the Bible. As it opens, God explained to Joshua how to lead the Israelite people.

Here is the beginning of the Book of **Joshua:**

After the death of God's servant Moses, God said to Moses' assistant, Joshua son of Nun: "My servant Moses is dead. Now it is time for you and all these people to cross the Jordan River into the land I am giving to them. I will give you every place where you set your foot, as I promised Moses. Your territory will reach from the desert to Lebanon, and from the great Euphrates River to the Great Sea on the west.

"No one will be able to stand up against you for your entire life. I will be with you as I was with Moses. I will never leave you nor forget you.

"Be strong and courageous, because you will lead these people to inherit the land I promised to their ancestors.

"Be strong and very courageous. Be careful to obey all the Torah Moses gave you. Do not let this Book of Torah depart from your mouth. Read it day and night, so that you may be careful to do everything written in it. Then you will be prosperous and successful. Have I not commanded you? Be strong and coura-geous. Do not be terrified; do not be dis-couraged, because God will be with you wherever you go."

So Joshua ordered the leaders of the people:

"Go through the camp and tell the people to get ready. In three days we will cross the Jordan and take hold of the land God is giving to us."…

They answered Joshua, "We will do whatever you command us. We will go wherever you send us. We will obey you just as we obeyed Moses, because God is with you as God was with Moses. Be strong and courageous!"

JOSHUA 1:1–11, 16–18

16

# The Promised Land

Read over the first paragraph of the *Tanakh* text. Draw an arrow on the map showing the approximate place where the Israelites would cross into the land that God promised them.

Find and mark with your pen or pencil where you think the borders should be, according to the *Tanakh* text, of the land promised by God.

# Conquest of Canaan

The word "conquest" means taking over a land and making it one's own. When a land is conquered, what happens to the people who were living there before? Sometimes they must move out and find a new place to live. Sometimes they join together with the conquerors. Sometimes they are killed or made slaves.

People today feel differently about conquest than did people a hundred years ago. We think of conquest as unfair, taking what is not ours, stealing other peoples' land and culture.

When we read the stories of the Israelites conquering the land of Canaan, it is easy for us to be embarrassed or uncomfortable, just as North Americans sometimes feel about the way settlers from Europe took away Native American land and culture.

The people who wrote the Books of **Joshua** and **Judges** saw things differently. They were proud that the people of Israel were strong and that their God—our God—was victorious over the gods of the other nations. They believed that God was on their side.

It is important for us to remember:

- We should not be quick to judge people of the past by the same standards we have today.

- The "conquest" of Canaan was not always violent. Conquest often meant peaceful settlement and blending together of cultures. Many nations were happy to accept the Israelite God and beliefs.

- Some of the more violent stories were probably exaggerations. Recent archeological evidence shows that these stories of violent conquest are probably not historically accurate. If this is so, and the settling of the Israelites was mostly peaceful, then why do you think our ancestors told these stories of warfare?

  _____

  _____

- If Israel had **not** settled in Canaan, there might not be any Jews today. And since they all grew out of Judaism, then there would probably be no Christianity, no Islam, no Ten Commandments, and no monotheism.

Have you ever felt proud and embarrassed about something at the same time? Think of a time when you did something well, when you won, when you had good luck or success. How did it feel? How did it make you feel about your friends who were not successful?

_____

_____

## God's Instructions to Joshua

When the people Israel crossed into the land that God had promised them, they would begin building a nation. It would be a long, hard process.

In the Book of **Joshua,** God instructed Joshua how to lead the Israelites.

God repeated one phrase three times to Joshua. See if you can find that phrase and write it below. (Hint: the people repeat the phrase at the end of the *Tanakh* text on page 19.)

_____

_____

_____

Why do you think God repeated this message three times to Joshua? Imagine that you are saying these words to Joshua. How would you explain them?

_____

_____

_____

There is a section of the *Tanakh* text that is similar to a familiar text from **Deuteronomy.** Look at the two texts on the following page. You probably recognize the **Deuteronomy** text as part of the *Sh'ma* and *V'ahavta* prayer. Underline the sections from **Deuteronomy** that are similar to what God said to Joshua.

Do not let this Book of Torah depart from your mouth. Read it day and night, so that you may be careful to do everything written in it.

JOSHUA 1:8

Take to heart these instructions that I give you this day. Teach them to your children. Say them when you are sitting in your house, when you are going on your way, when you lie down, and when you get up.

DEUTERONOMY 6:6–7

Joshua was told to remember the Torah. Why do you think we find this reminder so soon after the ending chapter of the Torah?

_____

_____

God told Joshua: "Do not be terrified; do not be discouraged, because God will be with you wherever you go."

When the text says, "God will be with you," what do you think that means? Will God actually be walking with Joshua? Do the words have another meaning?

_____

_____

How will knowing that God is with him help Joshua from becoming afraid or discouraged?

_____

_____

*Joshua was the first leader of the Israelite people when they entered the land promised by God. Joshua was a prophet who told the people Israel the words of God. The message of Joshua was that Israel must be strong and courageous as they entered the land. In the next chapter, we will read how Joshua and the Israelites began their conquest of the land.*

# Chapter Three

## THE WALLS OF JERICHO

*In this chapter, we will read a story that tells how the Israelites conquered a powerful city, and we will learn about a brave woman who went against the laws of her own people to do what she knew was right.*

# Walled Cities

In ancient times, cities were built with high stone walls around them. People could enter and leave the city through several gates, which were often guarded to keep intruders or invading armies out. (In North America during the time of the Wild West, people in the frontiers sometimes lived in walled forts made of wood.) The area just inside these gates was often a busy gathering spot. People would meet their friends, buy food and clothing from vendors, and eat at the city gate. Jerusalem, Rhodes, and London are some cities where the ancient walls still stand today.

The city walls served many purposes. These walls were usually very thick, with two layers of stones and a space between the layers where rooms and homes were built, like modern apartments. Walkways ran along the top of the wall, and soldiers often stood guard duty on these walkways, where they could watch out for invaders.

Jericho was such a city.

# Jericho

The town of Jericho is one of the oldest cities in the world. People were probably living there as long ago as 5000 B.C.E. Jericho sits in a river valley five miles from the Jordan River, to the north of the hot and desolate Dead Sea.

Joshua's first job as leader of Israel was to bring them across the Jordan River from the east and lead them into the land that God had promised them. While the people were still camped east of the river, Joshua made plans to begin taking possession of the land. His first goal was to take the city of Jericho.

Joshua son of Nun sent two spies from Shittim to look over the land. "Find out about Jericho," he told them. So they came to the house of a woman named Rahab and stayed there.

But someone told the king of Jericho that the Israelites had come to look at their land. So he sent his men to Rahab, ordering her to bring out the spies.

Rahab had already hidden the men. She told the guards, "Yes, they were here. But I didn't know where they were from. They left a just a little while ago. I don't know where they went. You better go after them. You might catch up with them if you hurry."

All this time, the spies were up on the roof, hidden under stalks of grain. The king's men set out after the spies, going toward the Jordan River. The city gate closed behind them.

Later, Rahab went up on the roof and said to the spies, "I know that God has given this land to you, and the people here are very concerned. We heard how God split the Sea of Reeds when you left Egypt. When we heard about it, we were frightened because your God is everywhere. Please promise me that you will be kind to my family, because I have shown kindness to you. Promise that you will spare the lives of my father and mother, brothers and sisters and their families, and that you will save us from death."

"Our lives for your lives!" the men assured her. "If you don't turn us in, we will treat you kindly and faithfully when God gives us the land."

So she let them down by a rope through the window. Her house was part of the outer city wall.

She told them, "Go to the hills so they won't find you. Hide there for three days, and then go on your way."

The men said to her, "Put this red ribbon on your window. Have your whole family come stay with you at your house. That way we can keep our promise. We can't be responsible for their safety if they leave your house and go out into the street."

She agreed with everything they said. So she sent them off and put a red ribbon on the window. They went into the hills and stayed there three days, until the king's men had searched all along the road and returned without finding them.

The two men started back. They went down across the river and came to Joshua and told him everything that had happened to them.

They said to Joshua, "God is certainly giving the whole land to us; all the people are afraid of us."

JOSHUA 2:1–24

The story that you just read is one of the many texts that you will be looking at. These sections of text are taken from the *Tanakh* and translated from Hebrew specifically for this book. At the end of each *Tanakh* text, you will find a name and some numbers. We call these "citations." The citation tells us where we can find that text in any edition of the Bible. In the above case, the citation is:

JOSHUA 2:1–24

This tells us that the text comes from the book of **Joshua,** chapter 2, and verses 1 through 24 of that chapter.

Below are three verses taken from various places in the *Tanakh*. Each one is followed by its citation. In the spaces provided, fill in the book, chapter, and verse.

| TEXT | BOOK | CHAPTER | VERSE |
|---|---|---|---|
| On the seventh day God finished the work that God had been doing, and rested on the seventh day from all the work God had done.<br>GENESIS 2:2 | | | |
| Be holy, for I, Adonai your God, am holy.<br>LEVITICUS 19:2 | | | |
| It is a tree of life to those who hold fast to it.<br>PROVERBS 3:18 | | | |

# The Faith of Rahab

In the text, Rahab disobeyed the law of Jericho by helping the spies. If she had been caught, she would have been guilty of treason. It seems strange that this woman would risk her life to protect two men from a different nation.

As we read texts from the Bible, a good first step is to understand what the writer wanted to tell us. In this story, the author is telling us that two spies came to Jericho and were protected by a woman name Rahab. Our first task is to discover the straightforward meaning of the story as it was written. In Hebrew this is called the *p'shat* פְּשָׁט, meaning the "plain sense." *P'shat* is like a newspaper summary of the events that happened.

The text gives us a *p'shat* reason why Rahab protected the spies. Look over the text, and write the *p'shat* explanation in the space below.

According to the text, Rahab protected the spies because...

_____

_____

_____

_____

After finding the *p'shat,* it sometimes helps to try to understand **why** the author wrote what he or she did. The Hebrew word for this is *kavanah,* which means "motive" or "intention." Discovering the *kavanah* is not as simple as finding the *p'shat.* You can't always find the answer in the text itself.

In the space below, write why the author of the story might have chosen to have a non-Israelite woman protect the spies. Why might this have been important to the author?

The author had Rahab protect the spies in order to show...

_____

_____

_____

_____

How do you think Rahab viewed the Israelites? As good or bad? Strong or weak? Mean or merciful? What else?

_____

_____

_____

# The Walls Came Tumbling Down

In the following text we are told of an amazing and miraculous event. The Israelites, with God's help, conquered the city of Jericho, making the very walls of the city crumble.

The city of Jericho was locked tight to keep the Israelites out. God said to Joshua, "I will help you conquer Jericho. Have your army march around the city once a day for the next six days. At the center of the army, seven priests carrying shofars should march in front of the Ark.

"On the seventh day, have them march seven times around the city, with the priests blowing their shofars. When you hear the long blast, have all the people shout. The wall of the city will collapse, and your people will enter."

So Joshua told the priests, "Get the Ark of God's Covenant and have seven priests carry shofars in front of it. Go and march around the city, with soldiers going ahead of the Ark of God."

When Joshua had spoken, the people followed the instructions. Part of the army marched ahead of the priests who blew the shofars, and the rest of the soldiers followed the Ark. The priests blew the shofars, but Joshua reminded the people, "Do not give a war cry or raise your voices, do not say a word until the day I tell you to shout."

The Israelites did this for six days, carrying the Ark of God in a circle, once around the city.

On the seventh day, the people got up at daybreak and marched around the city as they had before, only this time they circled the city seven times. And on the seventh time around, the priests blew on their shofars.

Joshua said, "Shout! God has given you the city! The city and everything in it are for God. Spare Rahab and anyone who is with her in her house, because she protected our spies. All the silver and gold and bronze and iron items belong to God. No one is to take them."

When the shofars sounded, the people yelled. And amidst the noise of shouts and shofar blasts, the walls of Jericho collapsed. The Israelites charged in and took the city. They devoted the city to God and destroyed with the sword every living thing in it—men and women, young and old, cattle, sheep and donkeys.

Joshua told the two spies, "Go to Rahab's house. Bring her and everyone with her out here."

So they brought Rahab, her father and mother, and her entire family to a place near the Israelite camp. Then they destroyed the entire city and everything in it, except for the silver and gold and metal items that they put in God's treasury.

Joshua spared Rahab and her family because she hid the men Joshua had sent as spies to Jericho. She lives among the Israelites to this day.

Then Joshua made this promise: "Anyone who tries to rebuild Jericho shall be cursed by God. His people will die as he lays its foundations; they will die as he sets up its gates."

God was with Joshua, and he was famous throughout the land.

JOSHUA 6:1–27

The above text tells us that the walls of Jericho were destroyed because of the marching, yelling, and shofar blowing of the Israelites. Like the parting of the Sea of Reeds for Moses, this is a miracle on a grand scale. We will be finding many miracles in the stories of the judges of Israel.

There have been many explanations for the destruction of the walls of Jericho:

- Perhaps a natural event like an earthquake caused the walls to collapse.

- Perhaps the walls were weak, and the noise of the Israelites struck just the right sonic frequency to shatter the walls.

- Perhaps the hand of God helped knock down the walls.

- Perhaps the Israelites stormed the city in a normal attack and later knocked down the walls.

- Some historians think that at the time Joshua was leading the Israelites, Jericho was already an empty ghost town and its walls had crumbled long before.

Whatever the actual explanation is, the person who wrote the story of Joshua and Jericho wanted us to believe that the marching and the shofar blasts had a miraculous effect.

Can you think of a reason why the author wrote the story in this way? What might have been the author's purpose for telling us about the miracles?

_____

_____

_____

Today Jews associate the blowing of the shofar with Rosh HaShanah. The blast of the shofar has been called "a wake-up call for the soul." What do you think that means?

_____

_____

_____

How does it make you feel when you listen to the blasts of the shofar?

_____

_____

_____

It was the custom in ancient times that after an army conquered another city, the victorious soldiers would take everything of value that they could carry out. In English, we call this "booty," "plunder," and the "spoils of war." The Israelites were specifically told that they were not to plunder Jericho. "All the silver and gold and bronze and iron items belong to God," they were told. "No one is to take them." How can you explain this? Why were the Israelites not allowed to profit from the spoils of Jericho?

_____

_____

_____

# The Day the Sun Stood Still

Jericho wasn't the only miracle that helped Israel during the time of Joshua. One of the most famous occurred when the Israelites were battling the Amorites to help the people of Gibeon. The Israelites were winning, but the battle hadn't finished when the sun began setting on the horizon. In order to continue the battle by daylight, Joshua ordered the sun to stand still.

After the events at Jericho, the people of Gibeon, a town west of Jericho, became friends and allies with Israel. When five Amorite cities attacked Gibeon, the Gibeonites asked for help from Joshua.

It was common for each large city to have its own king. The kings of these five cities are called "Amorite" kings. Historians don't know for certain why the author of **Joshua** called them Amorites. The Amorites were one of the nations living in Canaan long before Joshua brought the Israelites into Canaan. Perhaps the author used the word "Amorites" as a synonym for "Canaanites." Or perhaps these five kings had historical ties to old Amorite dynasties found in Syria and Iraq centuries earlier.

The text tells us:

The five Amorite kings—the king of Jerusalem, the king of Hebron, the king of Jarmuth, the king of Lachish, and the king of Eglon, with all their armies—joined together and attacked Gibeon. The people of Gibeon sent word to Joshua who was camped at Gilgal, "Please don't fail us. We are your servants. Come quickly and help us. The Amorite kings have come down from the hills to attack us." So Joshua brought his entire army up from Gilgal.

God said to Joshua, "Do not be afraid of them, for I will deliver them into your hands."

Joshua marched all night from Gilgal to make a surprise attack. God caused the Amorites to be so frightened that they retreated from Gibeon. The Israelites chased them all the way to Azekah and Makkedah. During the chase, God made huge hailstones fall from the sky onto the Amorites. More died from the hailstones than from Israelite weapons.

During this chase, Joshua called out to God in front of all the Israelites:

*"Stand still, you sun, at Gibeon,*
*Moon stop in the Aijalon Valley!"*
*The sun stood still*
*And the moon stopped.*
*While one nation defeated their*
*   enemies.*

As it is written in the Book of the Upright: The sun stood still in the sky, and did not set for a whole day, because God was on the side of Israel. Never before and never since has there ever been a time like that when God listened to the words of a man.

JOSHUA 10:5–14

*When Joshua brought the Israelites over the mountains into Canaan, they were a weak, new presence in the region. By the time of Joshua's death, the Israelites ruled numerous cities, and several nations had joined up with them and their God. Joshua marked the beginning of the age of the judges: a time of great miracles and brave heroism, and the land that had been Canaan became the land of Israel. In chapter 4, we will read more of these events as we begin looking at the Book of **Judges**.*

# Chapter Four

# JUDGES: DEBORAH AND GIDEON

*While the people of Israel were wandering in the desert, they needed a leader who would hold them together, see to their survival, and teach them God's laws. Once they crossed into Canaan, Israel needed a new kind of leader, one who would lead them against their enemies and guide them in building a new nation. The Israelites called these new leaders shoftim, or "judges." In this chapter, we will read about the deeds of two judges, Deborah and Gideon.*

The Israelites who came into Canaan with Joshua were not a unified nation. They were a band of twelve tribes linked by a common past and a common God. Once they entered the land, each tribe dispersed into its own territory. These twelve separate states were something like the American states and Canadian provinces would be if there were no national governments.

# The Tribes of Israel

### Were There Really Twelve Tribes?

The number twelve is a favorite among the ancient Hebrew writers. There are twelve months, twelve signs of the Zodiac *(mazal)*, the twelve sons of Jacob, and in one tradition, twelve judges who judged over Israel. The twelve tribes of Israel correspond to Jacob's twelve sons.

But the lines are not always clear. Sometimes twelve doesn't add up to twelve. For instance, there is no tribe of Joseph, but two tribes named for his sons Ephraim and Manasseh. The tribe of Simeon merged in with Judah, and the tribe of Levi didn't have a territory, but acted as priests throughout the land.

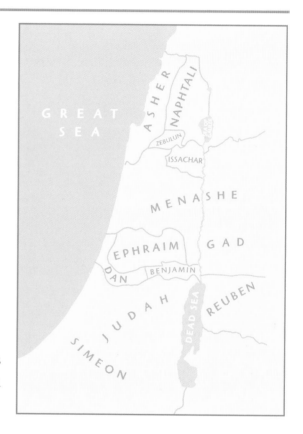

We call the individual groups of Israelites "tribes"—or *shevatim* (singular, shevet) in Hebrew. What exactly was a tribe

In the ancient Middle East, a large number of families would band together—they would live near each other, work together, and help each other when there was a threat. Even if the different families in this group were not related, they would have said that they were all descended from the same ancestor.

There were twelve such groups in ancient Israel: the twelve tribes, or *shivtei-Yisrael* שִׁבְטֵי יִשְׂרָאֵל. At first they were named for the twelve sons of Jacob: Reuben, Simeon, Levi, Judah, Issachar, Zebulun, Gad, Asher, Dan, Naphtali, Benjamin, and Joseph's two sons Ephraim and Manasseh.

# What Is a Judge?

For us, the word "judge" means a very specific role: a public official whose job is to resolve problems brought before a court. He or she is a legal referee who listens to two sides of an argument or dispute and then decides the outcome: who is right, who is wrong, who is responsible, and what penalty or punishment is appropriate.

For ancient Israelites living three thousand years ago (around 1100 B.C.E.), "judge" had a very different meaning. The Hebrew word for judge—*shofet* שׁוֹפֵט—meant someone who served the people as governor, lawgiver, captain, and head of a court.

This was a very difficult time for the young Israelite nation. The Exodus from Egypt unified Israel. The people shared common goals: to survive the wilderness of Sinai, to reach Canaan, and to be a free nation. But after the death of Moses and then Joshua, the Israelites spread to different regions of Canaan and faced many other nations, some friendly and some warring.

The *shoftim* (plural of *shofet*) were a new kind of leader. They were strong military chiefs who could rally groups of tribes together. Many of the judges were also prophets—someone through whom God speaks.

In this next text, we begin the Book of **Judges:**

After the death of Joshua, the Israelites asked God, "Who will lead us in the fight against the Canaanites?"

God answered, "The people of the tribe of Judah. I have given the land to them."

Then the tribe of Judah invited the members of the tribe of Simeon, "Join us as we go into the land and fight against the Canaanites. We'll help you claim your own territory."

So the tribe of Simeon went with them. When Judah attacked, God gave the Canaanites and Perizzites into their hands, and they struck down ten thousand men at Bezek.

JUDGES 1:1–4

# "The Israelites Did What Was Offensive to God"

How do we respond when we lose games, sports events, or other competitions? First we might become angry or disappointed. Then we might blame our loss on bad luck, bad weather, or an opponent who cheats. We might blame it on our own lack of energy, intelligence, or practice.

For most of the writers of the early Bible books—including *N'vi-im*—there was a clear-cut explanation for any lost battle or failed harvest: the people must have done something offensive to God.

In the previous chapter, we read how Rahab believed that God was with the Israelites. For much of ancient Israel's history, the people were falling into and out of God's favor. The Hebrew term for this is *motzei chein b'einei Elohim*—to find grace in God's eyes.

In the next passage, we will read about how Israel lost favor with God. They did evil in God's eyes: *vayaasu ra b'einei Adonai*.

Another generation arose, which had not experienced God or that which God did for Israel. And the Israelites did what was offensive to God. They worshiped the Baalim and forgot the God of their ancestors, who had brought them out of the land of Egypt. They followed other gods, from among the gods of the people around them, and bowed down to them. They provoked God. They ignored God and worshiped Baal and Ashtaroth. And God grew very angry at Israel and handed them over to their enemies. In every battle they waged, God allowed their enemies to defeat them.

JUDGES 2:10–15

The author described the sin of the Israelites as worshiping "Baalim" and "Ashtaroth." The word "Baal" means "lord" or "master," and the Israelites used it to refer to any of the male foreign gods. "Baal" could be Asshur the god of Assyria, or Marduk the god of Babylon.

The word "Ashtaroth" (sometimes "Asherah") referred to the many female fertility gods that people worshiped. She had many names, including Astarte and Ishtar.

In the next chapter of **Judges,** we learn more about what sort of behavior made God angry at the Israelites:

Jewish Astarte, Gaza, Ivory, 8th Century B.C.E. Photograph by Erich Lessing from Art Resource, NY.

The Israelites lived among the Canaanites, Hittites, Amorites, Perizzites, Hivites, and Jebusites. They took their daughters in marriage and gave their own daughters to their sons, and served their gods. The Israelites did evil in the eyes of God; they forgot God and served the Baalim and the Asherahs. God became angry at Israel and made them subjects of Cushan-rishathaim, king of Aram-naharaim, for eight years.

JUDGES 3:5–8

As we read these stories, we can learn a lot about how the ancient Israelites lived and what they believed.

While reading these texts from the *Tanakh,* it is important to remember that there was a person writing this down thousands of years ago. That writer held beliefs and attitudes. By carefully reading the above texts, we can understand how the writers of the Book of **Judges** thought the Israelites should behave.

What was the author's purpose? Reread the last two sections of text. List four things the Israelites did that "angered God" from the many sins listed in the texts.

_____

_____

_____

# Deborah

After Joshua, one of the first judges we read about is a woman named Deborah. The writer of **Judges** tells us that Deborah was a prophet and a judge. Deborah was a wise and brave leader, who helped an Israelite general named Barak to defeat a Canaanite army.

One of the more surprising stories in this battle is a frightening and brave act by another woman, Jael, who murdered the enemy captain.

The Israelites were under the power of King Jabin of Canaan, whose army commander was Sisera. The Israelites cried out to God, because Sisera had ruthlessly oppressed them for twenty years.

Deborah, wife of Lappidoth, was a prophet. She led Israel at that time. She used to sit under the Palm of Deborah, between Ramah and Bethel in the hill country, and the Israelites would come to her for decisions.

She summoned Barak son of Abinoam and said to him, "God has commanded that you go march up to Mount Tabor with ten thousand soldiers. God will make Sisera and his chariots and troops come toward you, and at Wadi Kishon God will deliver Sisera into your hands."

Barak said, "I will only go if you come with me. If not, I will not go."

"Very well, I will go with you," she answered. "But if so, it might be embarrassing for you when everyone watches God deliver Sisera into the hands of a woman."...

Sisera heard that Barak son of Abinoam had gone up to Mount Tabor.... He fled on foot and hid in the tent of Jael, wife of Heber the Kenite, who was a friend of King Jabin. Jael invited him into her tent and covered him with a blanket. He said, "Please give me some water. I'm thirsty." She served him some milk and then covered him up again. He said, "Stand at the entrance, and if anyone comes, tell them no one is here." Then Jael wife of Heber took a tent pin and a hammer. When Sisera was fast asleep from exhaustion, she sneaked up and drove the tent pin through his head.

JUDGES 4:2–9, 12, 17–21

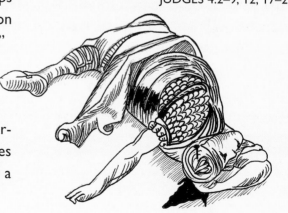

The text describes Deborah as sitting under "the Palm of Deborah." The tree is an important image in the *Tanakh*. The tree in this text is called *Tomer D'vorah* in Hebrew. It was probably a date palm. We also find throughout the *Tanakh* references to huge trees or tree groves called "terebinths" in English (*eilah* or *eilon* in Hebrew).

We find trees in the religions of other cultures as well. In ancient Britain and in northern Europe, trees were the object of worship, especially the oak tree among the Druids. In the Far East, it was while sitting in the shade of a Bodhi tree that the Buddha became enlightened. Trees often represent wisdom and teaching. Can you think of any other trees that appear in the *Tanakh?*

_____

_____

Why are trees used as a symbol for wisdom and teaching? Why do you think this is such a common image?

_____

_____

What did Jael do to help save the Israelites from the Canaanite commander Sisera?

_____

_____

As we read this story today, it is hard to imagine killing someone in this manner. To us it may seem cruel and brutal. But to the Israelites, Jael was considered a great hero for what she had done. How do you think the Israelites viewed Jael's behavior? Why would they see her as a brave hero?

_____

_____

_____

# The Song of Deborah

Following the battle against Sisera's army, the Israelites celebrated and honored the brave men and women who risked their lives.

Although the Book of **Judges** was probably written long after the events actually happened, the author of **Judges** included a poem that many historians think is the oldest piece of writing in the Bible. The judge Deborah may have actually written this poem, celebrating the battle at Mount Tabor.

Imagine, a woman may have written the oldest section of the Bible!

On that day Deborah and Barak son of Abinoam sang this song:

................................................

*Hear, kings! Listen, rulers! I sing to God, I sing;*
*I play music to the God of Israel.*

................................................

*Listen to the singers at the watering places.*
*They tell stories of the righteous acts of God,*
*the righteous acts of his warriors in Israel.*

................................................

*Most blessed of women be Jael,*
*Wife of Heber the Kenite,*
*Most blessed of tent-dwelling women.*
*He asked for water, and she gave him milk;*

*In a bowl fit for nobles*
*She brought him curdled milk.*

*Her hand reached for the tent peg,*
*Her right hand for the workmen's hammer.*
*She struck Sisera, she crushed his head,*
*She shattered and pierced his temple.*
*At her feet he sank, he fell; there he lay.*
*At her feet he sank, he fell; where he sank,*
*There he fell—dead.*

................................................

*So may all your enemies perish, O God!*
*But may they who love you be like the sun*
*When it rises in its strength.*

                                    JUDGES 5:1, 3, 11, 24–27, 31

Under the leadership of Deborah and other strong leaders, Israel dwelled peacefully in the land of Canaan, growing in numbers while living tranquilly beside their neighbors. But as we've seen before, the peace did not last. We learn from the text that forty years after the defeat of Sisera's army under Deborah, Israel was attacked by the Kedemites, the Midianites, and one of their fiercest enemies, the Amalekites.

# Gideon Son of Joash

Gideon was a modest and humble man who used his cleverness and ingenuity to lead Israel against the Midianites.

The Israelites did what was offensive to God, and God delivered them into the hands of the Midianites for seven years.…

An angel of God came and sat under the terebinth at Ophrah, which belonged to Joash the Abiezrite. His son Gideon was then beating out wheat inside a winepress in order to keep it safe from the Midianites. The angel of God appeared to him and said, "God is with you, valiant warrior!"

Gideon said, "Please, sir. If God is with us, then why have all these terrible things happened to us? Where are God's wondrous deeds about which our parents told us? They told us that God brought us out of Egypt. But now God has abandoned us and delivered us into the hands of Midian!"

He said, "You have the strength to save Israel from the Midianites. I now make you God's messenger."

He said, "Please, sir. How can I save Israel? My family is the lowest in the tribe of Manasseh, and I am the youngest of my father's family."

He answered, "I will be with you. And you shall defeat the Midianites."

JUDGES 6:1, 11–18

# Gideon's Trumpet

In one of Gideon's first adventures, he selected a tiny army—300 soldiers out of 3,200 who were prepared to go to battle with him. In a battle against a massive Midianite and Amalekite encampment, Gideon used horn blasts, as Joshua did at Jericho, to defeat his enemies. Instead of using the sound to break down city walls, Gideon used the trumpet blasts to confuse his enemies and to give his own men confidence. These trumpets are one of the earliest uses of special effects.

The story of the battle begins with a tale of a dream:

The Midianites and the Amalekites, along with other Eastern nations, were camped in the valley, thick as locusts, with countless camels as numerous as the sands on the seashore.

At the Israelite camp, Gideon happened to overhear a man describing a dream to his friend. "I dreamt that a loaf of barley bread was rolling into the Midianite camp. It smashed into a tent so hard that the tent flipped over and collapsed."

His friend responded, "That can only mean the sword of Gideon son of Joash the Israelite. God has given Midian and all the camp into his hands."

After hearing the dream and its interpretation, Gideon bowed low. He returned to the camp of Israel and shouted, "Let's go! God has given the camp of Midian into your hands."

He divided the 300 men into three companies, and he put trumpets and empty pitchers into the hands of all of them, with torches inside the pitchers.

He said to them, "Watch me, and when I come to the outskirts of the camp, do as I do.

"When I and all who are with me blow the trumpet, then you also blow the trumpets all around the camp and say, 'For God and for Gideon.'"

So Gideon and the hundred men who were with him came to the outskirts of the camp at the beginning of the middle watch, when they had just posted the watch; and they blew the trumpets and smashed the pitchers that were in their hands.

When the three companies blew the trumpets and broke the pitchers, they held the torches in their left hands and the trumpets in their right hands for blowing, and cried, "A sword for God and for Gideon!"

Each stood in his place around the camp; and all the army ran, crying out as they fled.

When they blew 300 trumpets, God set the sword of one against another even throughout the whole army; and the army fled as far as Beth-shittah toward Zererah, as far as the edge of Abel-meholah, by Tabbath.

The men of Israel were summoned from Naphtali and Asher and all Manasseh, and they pursued Midian.

Gideon sent messengers throughout all the hill country of Ephraim, saying, "Come down against Midian and take the waters before them, as far as Beth-barah and the Jordan." So all the men of Ephraim were summoned, and they took the waters as far as Beth-barah and the Jordan.

They captured the two leaders of Midian, Oreb and Zeeb, and they killed Oreb at the rock of Oreb, and they killed Zeeb at the wine press of Zeeb, while they pursued Midian; and they brought the heads of Oreb and Zeeb to Gideon from across the Jordan.

JUDGES 7:12–25

*The stories of Deborah and Gideon help us to imagine the early years of the Israelite nation as a time of bravery and of miracles. In the next chapter, we will be learning about the strangest judge of them all—Samson.*

# Chapter Five

# SAMSON: THE WARRIOR JUDGE

*In the last chapter, we read about Deborah and Gideon, two brave judges who used their wisdom and personal strength to lead Israel. In this chapter, we will read about a very different kind of hero. Samson was hardly wise, and he was not a leader. But he was strong, and the spirit of God helped him fight against the Philistines for the people Israel.*

How can we understand the story of Samson? Judges were thoughtful, wise, and clever people who worked well with other people. Samson, by contrast, was rough, hot-tempered, and wild. Unlike the other judges who led the people in battle, Samson always fought alone. And while we are told that Samson had the "spirit of God," he seemed to be more interested in women than in the good of Israel.

The story of Samson is a tale of miracles. It is hard to read about him without thinking of fantastic heroes like Superman or Hercules. His "heroic deeds" seem more appropriate to superhero comics than to the Bible. Samson's strength was miraculous (he drew his strength from his hair), and his very birth was miraculous:

The Israelites again did what was offensive to God, and God delivered them into the hands of the Philistines for forty years.

There was a certain man from Zorah, from the tribe of Dan, whose name was Manoah. He and his wife had not been able to have children. An angel of God appeared to his wife and said to her, "You are now barren and have borne no child. But you shall conceive and bear a son. Be careful not to drink wine or other intoxicants, or to eat anything unclean. Do not cut the hair of your son, for he will be a Nazir, and he shall be the first to deliver Israel from the Philistines."...

The woman bore a son, and she named him Samson. The boy grew up, and God blessed him. God's spirit began to move him at Camp Dan, between Zorah and Eshtaol.

JUDGES 13:1–5, 24–25

## Nazirites

In ancient Israel there were a certain group of people called Nazirites. We don't know very much about them. Any Israelite—man, woman, or child—could become a Nazir for any length of time. During the time a person is a Nazir, she or he may not drink wine or liquor, cut his or her hair, or come in contact with a dead body.

The role of Nazir seems similar to monks and nuns in the Catholic and Buddhist religions. A Nazir is a person who lives an especially spiritual life and is completely dedicated to God.

With that in mind, Samson was the most unlikely Nazir in all of Israel. He was violent, had a bad temper, liked to chase women, and probably drank a lot. He **did** keep his hair long. Perhaps that's why he was known as a Nazir. The author of **Judges** tells us that Samson had the spirit of God in him. But in the biblical text below, you will see that he was hardly a spiritual man:

Samson went to Timnah and saw a Philistine woman there. When he returned home he told his father and mother, "I saw a woman in Timnah, a daughter of the Philistines. Get her for me. I want to marry her."

His parents asked him, "Isn't there a woman from among our own people that you could marry? Don't take a wife from the uncircumcised Philistines."

But Samson told his father, "Get her for me. I like her looks."

His parents didn't realize that God was using this as a strategy against the Philistines, who at that time were ruling over Israel.

Samson went back to Timnah with his parents. When they came to the vineyards of Timnah, a young lion came roaring toward him. The spirit of God came to him, and he became so powerful that he tore the lion like one would tear a young goat through. He didn't tell his parents what had happened.

He went down and talked to the woman. She looked good to Samson. Later when he came to get her, he stopped to look at the lion carcass. He discovered a swarm of bees and honey inside the lion's body.

So he scraped the honey into his hands and went on, eating as he went. When he came to his father and mother, he gave some to them and they ate it; but he did not tell them that he had scraped the honey out of the body of the lion.

Samson then held a feast and invited some of his friends. Samson said, "I have a riddle for you…: "Out of the eater came something to eat, out of the strong came something sweet."

JUDGES 14:1–12, 14

What did Samson mean by his riddle "Out of the eater came something to eat, out of the strong came something sweet"?

_____

_____

Samson married the Philistine woman, but the marriage didn't last. Samson's friends tried for several days to guess his riddle. Eventually, Samson's wife gave in and told them the answer. Samson was so angry that he went into town and killed thirty Philistine men.

Some time later, Samson went to visit his wife, only to discover that she had married one of his wedding guests! Samson was so enraged that...

Samson caught three hundred foxes. He took torches and tied the tails of each pair of foxes together, and set a torch between each pair of tails. He lit the torches and set the foxes loose in the grain fields of the Philistines. They set fire to the stacked grain, the standing grain, the vineyards, and the olive trees.

JUDGES 15:4–5

## Samson the Superman

After the incident with the foxes, the Philistines were quite angry with Samson. They wanted to punish him, and if they couldn't get to Samson, they would take out their anger on the entire Israelite nation. So Samson allowed himself to be tied up with rope and taken to the Philistines at the town of Lehi.

When Samson came to Lehi, the Philistines shouted as they saw him. The spirit of God came to him, and the ropes on his arms fell away as though burned away, and he was free again.

He spotted a fresh jawbone from a dead donkey. He grabbed it and used it to kill a thousand men.

Samson said, "With the jawbone of an ass, mass upon mass! With the jawbone of an ass I killed a thousand men."

Then he threw the jawbone from his hand, and he named the place Ramath-Lehi ["Jawbone Hill"].

By then he was extremely thirsty, and he called out to God, "You let me have this big victory. Are You now going to let me die of thirst and fall into the hands of the uncircumcised?"

God split open a cavern in Lehi, and water came gushing out of it. When he drank, his strength returned and he felt fresh. So he named it En-Hakkore ["The Caller's Spring"], which is in Lehi to this day.

Samson judged Israel twenty years in the days of the Philistines.

JUDGES 15:14–20

# Samson and Delilah

The most famous story about Samson is of his relationship with the beautiful Delilah. This story, like the life of Samson, is hard to figure out. Is it supposed to be funny? Is it supposed to be tragic? Is it an adventure or a love story?

The Philistines hated Samson. They wanted him dead. But Samson was too strong for the Philistines to capture. And so a group of high-ranking Philistine officials bribed Delilah to find out where Samson got his strength and how he could be weakened.

Samson fell in love with a woman in the valley of Sorek. Her name was Delilah.

The Philistine leaders came to her and asked, "Seduce him, and find out where his great strength lies. Find out how we can capture him so that we can punish him. We will each give you eleven hundred pieces of silver."

So Delilah said to Samson, "Please tell me where your strength is from. How can you be weakened?"

Samson said to her, "If they tie me up with seven fresh cords that have not been dried, then I will be weak like any other man."

The Philistine leaders brought her seven fresh cords, not yet dried, and she tied him up with them.

Meanwhile there were men hiding in an inner room. She said, "The Philistines are here, Samson!" He snapped the cords as a piece of straw splits when it touches fire. The secret of his strength was not discovered.

Then Delilah said to Samson, "You tricked me. You lied to me. Please tell me how you can be trapped."

He said, "If they tie me up tight with new ropes that have never been used, then I will be weak like any other man."

Delilah took new ropes and tied him up. She said, "The Philistines are here, Samson!" For the men had been hiding in the inner room. But he snapped the ropes from his arms like a thread.

Then Delilah said, "You keep tricking me and telling me lies. Now tell me how you can be trapped."

He said, "Try weaving the seven locks of my hair with a web and fasten it with a peg on the wall, and I will be weak like any other man."

While he slept, Delilah took the seven locks of his hair and wove them with a web and fastened it to the peg and said, "The Philistines are here, Samson!"

He awoke from his sleep and pulled out the pin of the loom and the web.

She said, "You say you love me, but your heart is not there. You tricked me three times and have not told me where your strength is."

She kept pressing him day after day until she had worn him down. So eventually he told her the truth: "No blade has ever touched my head. I have been a Nazir to God since before I was born. If my hair is cut, my strength will leave me, and I will be weak like any other man."

Delilah realized that he had told her the truth, so she called the Philistine leaders and said, "Come up once more, for he finally told me the truth." The Philistines leaders came and brought her money.

While Samson slept on her knees, she called aloud to the man and then she shaved off the seven locks of his hair. She had weakened him and his strength had gone.

She said, "The Philistines are here, Samson!" And he awoke thinking, "I'll break free like the other times." But he didn't know that God had gone from him.

The Philistines grabbed him and gouged out his eyes. They brought him down to Gaza and shackled him with bronze chains, and they put him to work as a mill grinder in prison. Meanwhile, his hair began to grow back.

The Philistine leaders gathered to offer a sacrifice to their god Dagon and to celebrate that their enemy Samson was now in their custody.

The people gathered to see him, and sang songs of praise:

*"Our god gave our enemy into our hands,*
*The destroyer of our country,*
*Who has slain many of us."*

When their spirits were high, they said, "Call Samson here to entertain us." So they called Samson from the prison, and he entertained them. They made him stand between the pillars.

Then Samson said to the boy who was guiding him, "Take me to the pillars that support this building, so I can lean against them." The house was filled with men and women. All Philistine leaders were there. And about three thousand men and women were on the roof looking on while Samson was amusing them.

Then Samson called to God and said, "O God, please remember me and please give me my strength just this once, O God, so that I can get my revenge on the Philistines for taking out my eyes."

Samson grabbed onto the two central weight-bearing pillars and braced himself against them, one with his right hand and the other with his left. And Samson said, "Let me die with the Philistines!"

He pushed with all his might so that the house fell on the leaders and all the people who were there. He killed more people in his death than all those he killed during his life.

His brothers and the rest of his family came down to get his body. They brought him up and buried him between Zorah and Eshtaol in the tomb of Manoah his father. He had judged Israel for twenty years.

JUDGES 16:4–31

47

What sort of hero was Samson? His superhuman strength is obvious. It is a miracle that his strength came from his hair. But did his heroism go beyond physical strength? Immediately after the story of his birth, the text tells us:

God's spirit began to move him at Camp Dan, between Zorah and Eshtaol.

JUDGES 13:25

The Rabbis have understood this verse in many different ways. One Rabbi in the Talmud, Rabbi Isaac, interpreted the word *l'faamo* ("to move him") as meaning "to ring him." He explained, "God's Presence rang out for Samson like a loud bell." What do you think Rabbi Isaac meant by this? How does the sound of a loud bell affect us? Can God's spirit affect us in the same way?

_____

_____

How else do you think Samson was moved by the spirit of God?

_____

_____

The Rabbis also point out the words that Samson said before breaking down the walls of the Philistine temple:

"O God, please remember me and please give me my strength just this once."

JUDGES 16:28

According to the Rabbis in the Talmud, this was the only time Samson ever asked for help. He never even asked anyone to carry his staff for him.

Imagine that you were one of Samson's close friends, and after his death you were asked to write the words on his gravestone. What positive messages and memories would you write about him?

_____

_____

_____

# Understanding Delilah

### A Real-Life Delilah

Margaretha Zelle was born in Holland in 1876 and lived much of her youth in Indonesia, where she learned to dance in the exotic Oriental style. In 1905 she became a famous dancer in the theaters of Paris. Men would fall in love with her and tell her their secrets. Before and during World War I, the Germans hired her to get secrets from the French officials who spent time with her. She was known in those days as Mata Hari.

How are we to understand the character of Delilah? Was she evil, plotting against the man who loved her? Was she a hero to her people, working as a secret agent for the Philistines? Was she really in love with Samson and then forced to spy on him by the Philistines?

The Rabbis of the Talmud point out that her name was a play on words:

It is taught by Rav [Rabbi Abba Arika] that even if her name had not been Delilah, she would still have been Delilah, because she weakened [dildelah] Samson's strength, weakened his understanding, and weakened his merits.

BABYLONIAN TALMUD, SOTAH 9B

How was Delilah like Rahab, the woman from Jericho who helped the Israelite spies? List the similarities and differences of the two women in the spaces below:

| HOW WERE DELILAH AND RAHAB SIMILAR? | |
|---|---|
| Rahab | Delilah |
| | |

| HOW WERE DELILAH AND RAHAB DIFFERENT? | |
|---|---|
| Rahab | Delilah |
| | |

Imagine what would have happened had the Israelites captured Delilah and put her on trial for conspiracy, espionage, and kidnapping. How would Delilah explain herself? What reasons and explanations would she use for her defense?

_____

_____

_____

Samson's name—pronounced "Shimshon" שִׁמְשׁוֹן in Hebrew—is related to the Hebrew word for "sun" (shemesh שֶׁמֶשׁ). Some historians have suggested that the stories of Samson may be based on older legends about a Mesopotamian sun god. Samson reminds other people of the Greek legends of Hercules.

_Whatever the true meaning behind the stories of Samson, and despite his shortcomings, he remains a symbol of heroism and an object of pride for the Jewish people. His stories are also very entertaining. In the next chapter, we will get to know the last of the judges of Israel—Samuel._

# Chapter Six

# SAMUEL: THE TRAINING OF A JUDGE

*The last of the great judges was a man named Samuel. He was not only a judge, but he was also an important prophet and priest for the Israelite people. In this chapter, we will learn about how Samuel was to become a great leader and about the events that happened to the nation that Samuel led.*

# The Last of the Judges

The period of the judges began sometime around 1150 B.C.E. with the death of Joshua and lasted until Saul became king in 1028 B.C.E. The entire period of the judges was about 125 years. Samuel would be the last of the great judges of Israel. Like the judges before him, he was a military leader, a legal expert, and a religious leader. Samuel was also a prophet and a priest, and he led Israel into the era of kings.

A note about the texts: The Book of **Samuel** was originally considered a single Hebrew book. Because of its length, it was often written on two separate scrolls, and when the Septuagint—an important Greek translation of the Bible—was written, **Samuel** was divided into two separate books, called First and Second Books of the Kingdoms. What we today call **First** and **Second Kings** were called the Third and Fourth Books of the Kingdoms. The separation of the Book of **Samuel** made by the Septuagint is now called **First** and **Second Samuel**. In this textbook we will sometimes use Roman numerals (**I Samuel**, **II Samuel**, etc.) to indicate these books.

There is another book that tells the history of the same period as **Samuel** and **Kings**. The Book of **Chronicles** is part of the Writings (*K'tuvim*) section of the *Tanakh*. Like **Samuel** and **Kings,** it is divided into two separate sections: **First Chronicles** and **Second Chronicles.**

The Books of **Samuel** tell about Samuel as well as Israel's first two kings, Saul and David. The Books of **Kings** tell about the reign of King Solomon and the many kings of Israel and Judah who followed after his death.

The story of Samuel's birth is a miraculous one. See if it reminds you of other birth stories we've read.

There was a man from Ramathaim in the hill country of Ephraim whose name was Elkanah son of Jeroham. He had two wives, one named Hannah, the other named Peninnah. Peninnah had children, but Hannah was childless. It was Elkanah's custom to go to the sanctuary at Shiloh each year to worship and make offerings to God.... He would offer portions of the sacrifice to Peninnah and all her sons and daughters. But only one portion would go to Hannah—even though she was Elkanah's favorite wife—because she had no children.

Peninnah used to tease Hannah, saying that God had closed her womb. This happened year after year. Whenever they went to the House of God, Peninnah would tease her, and she would weep and not eat. Her husband Elkanah would say, "Hannah, why are you crying? Why aren't you eating? Why are you so sad? Don't you know that I care for you more than ten sons?"

Hannah got up after dinner one night at Shiloh. The priest Eli was sitting by the door of the sanctuary. In her sorrow, Hannah prayed to God, weeping all the while. And she vowed: "Oh God, if You will look upon my suffering and remember me—don't forget me—and give me a male child, I will dedicate him to You for all the days of his life. No razor shall ever touch his head."

As she was praying, Eli the priest was watching her mouth. Hannah prayed in her heart, moving her lips, although her voice could not be heard. Eli thought she was drunk. He said, "Don't make a drunken spectacle of yourself. Sober up!"

But Hannah said, "Oh no, sir. I am very depressed, but I haven't had any wine or beer. I've been pouring out my heart to God. Don't treat me like a drunk. I've only been speaking out of my great sadness."

"Then go in peace," said Eli. "And may God grant you what you asked."

So she left, and the next day they went back to Ramah. God remembered Hannah, and she became pregnant and had a son. She named him Samuel, because she asked [*shaah*] of God [*me-El*]....

When the boy was old enough, she took him up with her, along with offerings of a bull, flour, and wine, and brought him to the House of God at Shiloh. After sacrificing the bull, they brought the boy to Eli. She said, "Please, sir. I am the woman who stood here beside you and prayed to God. It was this boy I prayed for. God gave me what I asked. I must now lend him to God. For as long as he lives, he shall be dedicated to God."

I SAMUEL 1:1–20, 24–28

We can learn many things from this short tale. It teaches us about how the Israelites prayed, how they offered sacrifices, and how important children were to them.

At the beginning of the story, Hannah was unable to have children. This made her very sad. That Peninnah had many children and would tease her made it even worse for Hannah. Having children was very important to people in the ancient world. It was a sign of wealth and success. It was also a sign that God was showing favor to the parents.

Hebrew names have meanings. Sometimes the name of a character in a story tells us something about the character. Below are three of the characters from this story, along with the meanings of their names. In the space provided, explain each name according to the personality of the character.

| ELKANAH | HANNAH | PENINNAH |
|---|---|---|
| "God provides" | "Grace" or "favor" | "Pearl" or "coral" |
| | | |

The text tells us that the name Samuel means "she asked of God." In truth, the name means "His name is God." What do you think was the author's reason for explaining Samuel's name as he did?

_____

_____

# Offerings

Horned altar, Megiddo, c. 900 B.C.E. Photograph by Erich Lessing. Israel Museum, Jerusalem.

In the early years of the Israelite people, sacrifice was the most important religious activity that people observed. The word "sacrifice" comes from the Latin, meaning "to make holy."

There are many words for sacrifice in Hebrew. Two of the most common Hebrew terms are *zebach* זֶבַח (slaughter) and *Korban* קָרְבָּן (closeness). The word *zebach* reminds us that animals had to be killed and prepared in a special manner in order to be sacrificed. The Israelites rarely (if ever) ate meat except as part of a sacrifice. So one of the duties of the priests was to serve as butchers to prepare animal offerings.

*Korban* reminds us of the purpose of sacrifice: to become closer to God. What better way to get closer than by sharing a meal with God? Wine, fruit, grain, or meat would be brought to an altar, which is a large, stone barbecue. Usually a priest *(Kohein)* or Levite (member of the tribe of Levi) would help. The meal would be prepared, cooked on the altar, and a portion left on the altar for God. Meanwhile, the family who brought the offering would eat the meal and share it with the priests.

**If you could invite God for a meal, what would you serve?**

_____

_____

People today have a poor understanding of what sacrifice meant to the Israelites. To the modern eye, sacrifice seems cruel and wasteful. People assume that entire animals were burned during a sacrifice. In truth, only one kind of sacrifice, the *olah,* involved burning all or most of the animal on the altar. Most often, when meat or poultry were being offered, only the fat, the blood, and some of the innards would be burned whole. All the parts of the animal that people would normally eat would be used for a meal.

Festivals were a time of great picnics in which families would bring their offerings to the Temple and share a meal with God and with the priests.

# An Altar at Shiloh

At the time of the judges, there were several Israelite cities that had altars. These included Bethel, Gilgal, Gibeon, Ophrah, and Dan. The most popular altar was the one at Shiloh, about twenty miles north of Jerusalem. In fact, until King David made Jerusalem the capital of the Israelite kingdom, Shiloh was the most important place for sacrifices. When King Solomon built the Temple in Jerusalem, it became a law that Jerusalem was the only place where sacrifices to God could be offered. This was fine for the people of Judah. But for Israelites living to the north, this was inconvenient and unfair. They wanted to continue making offerings at Shiloh and other places, despite the law.

# A Priest in Training

As soon as he was old enough, Samuel went to work for Eli the priest at the sanctuary of Shiloh.

> Elkanah and Hannah returned to Ramah, and the boy entered the service of God under the priest Eli.... Samuel worked as an attendant, wearing a linen ephod. His mother would make a new robe for him every year and bring it to him when she made the pilgrimage with her husband to offer the annual sacrifice. Eli would bless Elkanah and Hannah and say, "May God grant you more children, since you have given so much to God." Then they would return home. God paid attention to Hannah, and she bore three sons and two daughters. Meanwhile, Samuel grew up in service to God.
>
> I SAMUEL 2:11, 18–21

The text tells us that Samuel grew up in service to God. This could mean one of several things. Does it mean he became a priest in training? If so, he would have to come from the tribe of Levi, and the text doesn't tell us that. We are told that his parents were from Ephraim territory. That suggests that he was from the tribe of Ephraim. But since Levi didn't have a territory, Samuel's family may well have been Levites or *Kohanim*. In fact, in the Book of **Chronicles,** where Samuel's family is also mentioned, they are reported to be Levites. Later in the story, when Samuel takes over some of the duties of Eli the priest, it seems like this is the case.

Samuel and Samson are similar names. Both Samuel's mother and Samson's parents took a vow that they would treat their sons as special. Samson became a Nazir. Samuel became a prophet and also performed some priestly functions. Both men were judges, and both were filled with the spirit of God.

From the reading we've already done, how is a person different when filled with the spirit of God?

_____

_____

Samuel and Samson may have both been judges, but they were different in nearly every other way. Before we begin reading any more about Samuel's life, how do you think he will be different from Samson? What do you already know about their differences?

_____

_____

In the following text, God called on Samuel. The priest Eli soon realized that Samuel was a very special boy.

Young Samuel was in the service of God under Eli. In those days, the word of God was rare; prophecy was not widespread. One day, Eli was asleep in his usual place; his eyes had begun to fail and he could barely see. The lamp of God had not yet gone out, and Samuel was sleeping in the sanctuary of God where the Ark of God was kept. God called out to Samuel. The boy said, "I'm coming," and ran to Eli. "Here I am. You called me."

Eli replied, "I didn't call you. Go back to sleep."

So Samuel went back and lay down. Again God called, "Samuel!"

Samuel rose and went again to Eli and said, "Here I am. You called me."

But Eli replied, "I didn't call you, my son. Now go back to sleep."

Samuel had never before experienced God; the word of God had not yet been revealed to him. So God called to Samuel a third time. He got up and went to Eli and said, "Here I am; you called me."

Then Eli understood that God was calling the boy. He said to Samuel, "Go lie down. If you are called again, you should say, 'Speak, O God, for your servant is listening.'" So Samuel went to his place and lay down.

God came and stood there. God called, "Samuel! Samuel!"

And Samuel answered, "Speak, for your servant is listening."

God said, "I will tell you something that will make the ears tingle. I will punish the house of Eli for all the bad things they have done as he watched, for the sacrilege committed by his sons that Eli did not condemn. The sins of the house of Eli can never be expiated by sacrifice or offering."

Samuel lay there until morning. He was afraid to tell Eli what he had heard. But Eli called on Samuel, and said, "Samuel, my son?"

And he said, "Here I am."

And Eli said, "What did God tell you? Tell me everything. Don't leave out a single word."

So Samuel told him everything, withholding nothing from him. And Eli said, "It's God. God will do what is the right thing."

I SAMUEL 3:1–18

## The Meaning of Samuel's Call

In the above passage, we first learn that Samuel was a prophet. He was special because he could hear the voice of God when no one else could.

The story is gentle and, in a way, funny. God called on Samuel three times. Each time, Samuel thought that it was Eli calling him. In legends and fairy tales—and in many stories in *Tanakh*—someone is given three tests or three chances.

Where else in the Bible does the number three have special meaning?

_____

_____

Think of two stories—one from the Bible and one from any other source—in which the hero is tested three times.

_____

_____

# The Ark of the Covenant of God

The Ark was a wooden chest that was covered in gold. It was about 2½ feet tall, 2½ feet wide, and 4 feet long. Inside the Ark—often called *Aron HaB'rit* אֲרוֹן הַבְּרִית, or Ark of the Covenant—it was believed that the Israelites kept the stones of the Torah that God had given Moses. In the section that follows, you will see that the Ark had special powers:

Samuel grew up and God was with him. He was very honest. The people of every corner of Israel knew that Samuel could be trusted as a prophet of God. God spoke to Samuel at Shiloh, and Samuel spoke to all Israel.

Israel marched out to fight against the Philistines. They camped near Eben-Ezer, and the Philistines camped at Aphek. The Philistines lined up against Israel and attacked. Israel was badly beaten by the Philistines, who killed about four thousand men on the battlefield.

When the elders of Israel learned about the defeat, they said, "Why did God let us be beaten by the Philistines today? Let's get the Ark of the Covenant from Shiloh so that God can be there with us and protect us from our enemies.

The two sons of Eli the priest, Hophni and Phinehas, brought the Ark to the Israelite camp. When it arrived, the people shouted so loud that the earth shook. The Philistines heard the shouting and wondered, "What is all that Hebrew shouting about?" When they learned that the Ark of God had come to the camp, they were very frightened, remembering what God had done to the Egyptians with the plagues. The Philistines fought and won, chasing the Israelites from their homes. Thirty thousand Israelite soldiers died there. The Ark of God was captured, and Eli's two sons, Hophni and Phinehas, were killed.

I SAMUEL 3:19–4:11

From the time the Ark was taken away from the Israelites, bad things began to happen wherever it went. In particular, a statue of one of the Philistine gods, Dagon, fell apart when the Ark entered its sanctuary. The Philistines tried to store the Ark elsewhere, but wherever it went, people became sick or died.

In 1981, Hollywood filmmaker Stephen Spielberg released his great adventure film *Raiders of the Lost Ark,* in which archeologist/adventurer Indiana Jones battled with Nazis who wanted the Ark of the Covenant to use its power as a weapon. In the film, the Nazis suffered the same fate as the Philistines who took the Ark.

Before long, the Philistines realized that the Ark would continue to bring them trouble until its return to the Israelites, as we learn from the following text.

## The Return of the Ark

The Ark of God stayed in the Philistine country for seven months. Then the Philistines asked their priests and prophets, "What shall we do with this Ark of God? Should we send it back where it belongs?" They answered, "Do not send it back without extra pay-ments."... So the Ark was packed on a wagon with items of gold and returned to the Israelites.

The people of Beth-Shemesh were harvesting wheat in the valley when they looked up and saw the Ark. They rejoiced when they saw it.

I SAMUEL 6:1–3, 10–13

*Samuel son of Elkanah and Hannah was the last of the judges of Israel. During his years as their leader, the Israelite nation grew and became a more stable presence in Canaan. Samuel was strong and honest, and like the judges who judged before him, he was filled with the spirit of God. In the next chapter, we will continue to learn about Samuel and how Israel was transformed from a nation to a kingdom.*

# Chapter Seven

# A KING FOR ISRAEL

*For the first two hundred years of their existence, the Israelites were led by religious and military leaders. They had local leaders as well, but their central leader was an invisible God, not human at all. In this chapter, we will watch the Israelites turn a corner and anoint a human king to rule over them. As the Israelites soon learned, a king they could see was not always the best ruler.*

You have probably seen pictures of kings and queens from the time you were a small child. Fairy tales and movies are filled with royalty. Kings and queens are not just in fairy tales. Countries like England, Denmark, and Jordan still have kings and queens.

What is a king? How did royalty first come about? What do we know about kings in the ancient Middle East?

The English word "monarchy" comes from a Latin root meaning "rule by one." A king or queen, then, is a "monarch." In the ancient world, a king was the one person who ruled over a nation. The Hebrew word for king is *melech,* which means "one who rules or owns."

In earliest times, people lived in small clans and tribes. One person, usually a strong male, would take the role of leader. As chief, he had the responsibility of protecting his tribe from danger. He would also often take the best property—food, clothing, home— of the tribe.

As tribes grew, they settled into cities. As the cities grew, so did the role of chief. At some point, when the leader of a city governed farms and villages beyond the walls of his own city, the leader became a king.

In the ancient Middle East, people had certain beliefs about their kings:
1.  The king was appointed by their god. In some kingdoms, such as Egypt, the people believed that their king was a god.
2.  The king was responsible for making sure his city was well fortified and for constructing public buildings including temples.
3.  The king had the power to take anything—money, food, building supplies, and labor—in order to build up his city and his army.
4.  Usually the role of king was passed from father to son. This is called a "dynasty" or a "hereditary monarchy."

Throughout their history up to this point, the Israelites had no king. Their knowledge of Egypt, where the king was often cruel, may have restrained the Israelite leaders from centralizing their government in the hands of one person. Saying that God ruled the people just as God ruled the world was their way of saying that they didn't believe in centralized government.

In Hebrew prayers, God is called *Melech haolam* מֶלֶךְ הָעוֹלָם (Ruler of the universe). In what ways is God like a king or queen?

_____

_____

_____

Now that the Israelites were settling into their territories, it was only a matter of time until they had a king like all the nations around them. According to the Book of **Samuel,** the people came to Samuel asking for a king, as we read in the following text:

Samuel was a judge for Israel his entire life. Each year he made the rounds, visiting the towns of Bethel, Gilgal, and Mizpah, acting as judge over Israel at all those places. Then he would return to Ramah, for his home was there, where he would also judge Israel. He built an altar there for God.

When Samuel grew old, he appointed his sons as judges over Israel. The name of his firstborn son was Joel, and his second son's name was Abijah. The sons did not follow in their father's ways. They were greedy, they accepted bribes, and they twisted justice.

All the leaders of Israel met with Samuel at Ramah. They said, "You have grown old, and your sons have not followed your ways. Please give us a king, to lead us like all the other nations."

Samuel wasn't happy about this. He prayed to God, and God answered Samuel: "Listen to everything that the people said. They aren't rejecting you. They are rejecting Me as their king. It is like everything else the people have done since I brought them out of Egypt. They reject Me and worship other gods. Listen to their demand, but warn them about the things that kings will do to them."

Samuel did as God had said. He told the people, "This king you want so badly, do you know what he will do? He will draft your sons into his army, making them chariot drivers, cavalry, and foot soldiers. He will make them plow and harvest his fields and make his weapons. He will take your daughters and make them his perfumers, cooks, and bakers. He will seize your best fields, vineyards, and olive groves and give them to his friends. He will take a tenth of everything you grow, your livestock, your flocks, and you will become his slaves. One day you will cry out because of this king you wanted. But God will not answer you that day."

The people wouldn't listen to Samuel's warning. "No," they said, "we must have a king so that we can be like other nations. We need a king to lead us and to fight our battles."

God said to Samuel, "Listen to their demands. Give them a king."

Then Samuel said to the people of Israel, "You can all go home."

I SAMUEL 7:15–8:22

Samuel provided the people with plenty of reasons not to have a king. List three of them below.

_____

_____

_____

## Keeping Up with the Neighbors

Have you ever wanted something that many of your friends had? Perhaps a game or a toy. Maybe a certain kind of music or brand of clothes. There may be a popular movie or TV program that your parents don't want you to see.

Peer pressure is hard to ignore. Peer pressure is a force that makes us want to have or do something simply because it seems everyone around us is. Often, we want this thing only because of peer pressure. Still, the pressure is real. Kids and adults all experience some peer pressure.

Can you think of an instance in your life when you wanted something because everyone around you had it or was doing it? Describe or draw a picture of it in the space below.

# Saul

The Israelites did get themselves a king. Or more precisely, Samuel got them a king with the help of God. The name of their king was Saul. Before he became king, Saul son of Kish was a farmer. When we first meet Saul, he is trying to find some of his father's donkeys that had gone astray.

Saul had heard about Samuel and knew that he was a great prophet who might help him locate his missing donkeys.

Before Saul arrived at Samuel's home, God revealed to Samuel, "At this time tomorrow I will send you a man from the territory of Benjamin. Anoint him ruler of My people Israel. He will rescue them from the hands of the Philistines. I have listened to my people; I have heard their complaints."

As soon as Samuel saw Saul, God announced to him, "This is the man that I told you would govern My people."

Saul approached Samuel and said, "Excuse me, do you know where the seer lives?"

Samuel answered, "I am the seer. Go on up to the shrine. You're having lunch with me. Tomorrow morning when I send you off, I will tell you whatever it is you want to know. But do not worry about your stray donkeys. They have been found. And what is it that all of Israel is asking? They want you and your family line."

Saul replied, "But I am from Benjamin, the smallest of the tribes of Israel, and my clan is the lowest in the tribe of Benjamin. Why are you saying this to me?"

I SAMUEL 9:15–21

# Anointing a King

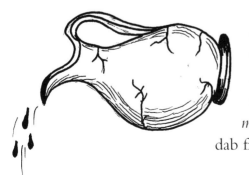

In modern Europe, when a person becomes king or queen, we say they have been "crowned" or that they have "taken the throne." The ceremony is called "coronation." The Israelite tradition for making someone king was called "anointing," or *mashach*. During anointing, a priest or a judge would dab fine olive oil on the head of the "anointed."

Samuel took a flask of oil and poured it on Saul's head. He kissed him and said "God hereby anoints you as ruler over His own people. When you leave me today, you will meet two men near Rachel's tomb who will tell you that your lost donkeys have been found.... After that you shall come to Givat HaElohim, where the Philistine troops are staying. When you arrive at the city, you will meet a group of prophets coming down from the high place with a lute, a tambourine, a flute, and a lyre, and they will prophesy. The spirit of God will come upon you and you will prophesy with them. You will become a different man...."

And so it happened that when Saul departed from Samuel, God gave him a new heart, and all those signs came to pass that day. And when they came to the hill, a group of prophets met him, and the spirit of God came upon him, and he prophesied with them. And so, whenever anyone who knew him before saw that he had prophesied with the prophets, they would say to each other, "What happened to the son of Kish? Is Saul now a prophet?"

I SAMUEL 10:1–2, 5–6, 9–11

In the previous text, Samuel told Saul that he would "become a different man." We are also told that "God gave him a new heart." Are we supposed to take these expressions literally? What do you think the text is telling us?

_____

_____

The text also tells us that the spirit of God came upon Saul and that he prophesied with the prophets. Explain what you think is meant by the phrase "the spirit of God came upon him."

_____

_____

Do you think you have ever felt the spirit of God? Is it possible for people today to feel that spirit just as the prophets did long ago? Where do you think this might happen to someone? What might happen to help a person feel that spirit? What do you think it would be like?

_____

_____

At first, Saul was very shy and modest about becoming king. After his anointing, Saul ran away and hid. But when he was finally brought to the people, they were happy, finally, to have a king.

Samuel called for Saul son of Kish, but no one could find him anywhere. They asked God, "Where is he? Have You seen him?"

And God responded, "He's there, among those containers."

So they went over and found him there, and they brought him to his place among the people. He was a head taller than anyone else.

Samuel said, "This is the one that God has chosen. There is no one like him among all the people."

And the people all shouted, "Long live the king!"

I SAMUEL 10:21–24

Saul ruled Israel for twenty-two years. During the final seven years, he ruled only over the northern tribes.

# Jonathan Son of Saul

Immediately after taking the throne, King Saul's first job was to protect the Israelite tribes from the invading Philistines. Saul had a son named Jonathan, who was always close to the side of his father. Jonathan was raised to be a strong military leader, and from a young age he led an army against the Philistines. Jonathan was a good person and a good leader. Saul hoped that his son would one day be king over Israel. Jonathan might have been a good king. He could be kind and strong. But he never had the chance to rule Israel.

As we will be reading in chapter 8, King David would become the next king. It will be interesting to keep in mind that David would be Jonathan's best friend and, at the same time, Saul's most important enemy.

# Saul Disappoints God

The Amalekite army was a rough band of pirate-like nomads from east of the Jordan River. Like the Philistines, they were one of Israel's fiercest enemies. It was typical of them to attack a city and plunder, or steal, all the wealth and goods they could take. God disapproves of the act of plunder. When war is necessary, it should be for the sake of justice. A war that is fought for personal gain is not a just war.

What reasons can you come up with for why it might be necessary to wage a war?

_____

_____

The judge/prophet Samuel gave King Saul specific instructions from God:

Samuel said to Saul, "I am the person God sent to anoint you as king over God's people Israel. Therefore, listen carefully to God's command.

"This is what God said: 'I am punishing the Amalekites for what they did to Israel, for attacking them on their way up from Egypt. Now go and attack Amalek, and kill them all. Spare no one. Kill men and women, children and babies, oxen, sheep, camels, and donkeys.'"...

Saul destroyed the Amalekite country and captured King Agag of Amalek alive. Saul had all the people killed, but he and his troops spared Agag, as well as all the good sheep, oxen, and other valuable livestock. They didn't kill everything, but only wiped out what was worthless to them.

God's word came to Samuel: "I regret that I made Saul king! He has ignored Me! He did not follow my instructions."...

Then Samuel said to Saul, "You may not seem like much to yourself, but you are the head of all the tribes of Israel. God anointed you king over Israel and sent you on a mission. God told you to wipe out the sinful Amalekites. Fight them until you have killed every one of them. Why did you disobey God and swoop down like a pirate stealing their spoils in God's sight?"

Saul tried to explain, "I did obey God. I captured King Agag of Amalek, and I wiped out the Amalekites. We took some of their best livestock. But I promise we will use some of it to make an offering to God at the altar of Gilgal." Samuel answered:

*"What do you think God prefers: Burnt offerings and sacrifices?*
*Or that we listen to his voice?*
*It is better to listen than to sacrifice.*
*Paying attention to God is more desirable than the fat of rams.*
*Because you have rejected God's command, God has rejected you as king!"*

I SAMUEL 15:1–3, 7–11, 17–23

The first thing we notice about this story is how violent God's instructions seem to be. Why would the same God who saved Israel from Egyptian slavery want them to destroy an entire nation? Why didn't God show mercy in this story?

_____

_____

_____

_____

# Sacrifices versus Mitzvot

The end of Samuel's speech to Saul is in the form of a poem. As we will see later in this book, many of the prophets gave their messages from God in the form of poetry.

In his poetic statement, Samuel asked Saul what is more important to God. What do you think God prefers: burnt offerings or observing the mitzvot?

_____

_____

_____

Priests and prophets, rabbis and scholars have long waged this debate. The sacrifices were a very important part of the Israelites' religious practice. But as time went on, study of Torah became more important for Jews. This was especially true after the Romans destroyed the Jerusalem Temple in 70 C.E.

In the space below, explain what you think God really wants from us. See if you can put it in terms of sacrifice versus mitzvot. (For an extra challenge, try writing your explanation in poetic verse as Samuel did.)

_____

_____

_____

_____

_____

_____

_____

_____

_____

_____

_____

_____

_____

*In this chapter, we learned how Israel became a kingdom, how its first king was chosen, and how God became disappointed in that king. In the next chapter, we will read about the next king to be chosen by God and how that man and King Saul became bitter enemies.*

# Chapter Eight

# SAUL AND DAVID

*Saul was soon to be replaced by the most famous of all Israelite kings. In this chapter, we will learn about the adventures, the intrigue, and the sadness that surrounded the first two kings of Israel.*

There are many stories about how David son of Jesse was chosen as king. David was a real, historical figure. We can be fairly certain of that. But from early times, the legends about him took on a life of their own. By the time the Book of **Samuel** was written down, there were several different stories about who David was and how he came to be king. The writers of **Samuel** did a good job weaving these stories together. But we are still left with some questions.

What did David do before he became king? Was he a shepherd? A musician? A soldier? Or was he really all three, as the text tells us?

When did David first meet Saul? We will see two different versions below. In one, David comes to work as a musician in Saul's palace. In the other version, David is the young sheepherder who kills the giant Goliath, and it seems that he and Saul are meeting again, for the first time.

In the following text, Samuel meets the next anointed one:

Samuel left for Ramah, and Saul went up to his home at Gibeah. Samuel never saw Saul again for the rest of his life. But Samuel never forgot how sad it was, how God made Saul king and then regretted it.

And God said to Samuel, "How long will you grieve over Saul? Get a container of oil and set out. I am sending you to Jesse of Bethlehem. I have decided that one of his sons will be king."

Samuel said, "How can I do that? If Saul finds out, he'll kill me."

God said, "Take a cow with you and invite Jesse to a sacrificial feast. Then I will show you the one that you shall anoint."

Samuel did as God told him. He went to Bethlehem and prepared for a sacrifice, and he invited Jesse and his sons to join him.

Samuel saw Jesse's son Eliab and thought, "He must be God's anointed."

But God told Samuel, "Pay no attention to his appearance or his tall stature. He is not the one I have chosen. God sees things differently than humans. A person sees only what is on the surface. God sees into the heart."

Jesse introduced his next son, Abinadab. But he was not the one God had chosen. Next, Jesse introduced Shammah, but God hadn't chosen him either. Jesse presented seven sons to Samuel, but he said, "God has not chosen any of these."

Then Samuel asked Jesse, "Are these the only sons you have?"

Jesse answered, "There is still the youngest. He is out tending the flock."

Samuel said, "Send someone to bring

him here. We shall not sit to eat until he gets here."

They brought the boy. He was red-cheeked, bright-eyed, and handsome. God said, "Now anoint him, for he is the one."

Samuel took his horn of oil and anointed the boy in the presence of his brothers. Then the spirit of God attached itself to David from that day forth.

Since God's spirit had departed from Saul, an evil spirit had begun to frighten him. His friends said, "This bad spirit is terrifying you. May we look for someone who is good at playing the lyre? Whenever the evil spirit comes over you, he will play it and you'll feel better."

Saul said, "Fine. Get someone who can play well."

One of his friends said, "Jesse of Bethlehem has a son whom I've heard. He's a very good musician, handsome, sensible, and strong. God is with him."

So Saul ordered Jesse to send him his son David. Jesse packed gifts for David to take to Saul. When David came to work for him, Saul liked him immediately and made him one of his guards. He told Jesse, "David will remain in my service. I like him."

Whenever Saul became angry, David would play the lyre, and Saul would relax and feel better. The evil spirit would leave him.

I SAMUEL 15:34–16:23

# How David Slew Goliath

One of the most famous stories about David is how he slew the giant Philistine, Goliath, with a stone and a sling. Goliath, according to our understanding of cubits and spans, must have been just under ten feet tall! It is no wonder that this story has become such an important symbol for the small and weak overcoming the large and mighty. In 1967, when the modern State of Israel defended herself against attacking Egyptian, Jordanian, Syrian, and Iraqi forces, many people saw it as a reenactment of the story of David and Goliath.

The Philistines assembled their army for battle. Saul and the men of Israel gathered and set up camp in the valley of Elah, preparing for battle.

The Philistines stationed on one hill, and Israel on the other. A Philistine hero stepped forward. His name was Goliath of Gath. He was six cubits and a span tall. He wore a bronze helmet and a heavy armored breastplate. He carried a javelin and a long spear.

He stood in front of the Israelite army

and called out, "What do you think you're doing challenging us? I am the Philistine champion. Choose one of your men and have him fight me. If he beats me and kills me, we will be your slaves. But if I beat him, then you shall become our slaves and servants...."

When Saul and all Israel heard what the Philistine said, they were terror stricken.

David was the youngest son of Jesse of Bethlehem. Three of his older brothers were with Saul at battle.... Jesse told David, "Take these provisions to your brothers. Take them quickly to them at the camp. Take these ten cakes of cheese to their captain. Find out how your brothers are doing. Bring me some word from them."

I SAMUEL 17:1–19, 11–13, 17–18

David arrived on the battlefield just in time to hear the giant Philistine repeating his challenge. David came to King Saul and said:

"Don't worry about a thing. I will go and fight the Philistine."

But Saul said to David, "You cannot go to that Philistine and fight him. You are just a boy. He's been a warrior all his life."

David replied to Saul, "I'm a shepherd for my father. If a lion or bear tries to make off with an animal from the flock, I would go after it and fight it and rescue the animal from its mouth. If it attacked me, I would grab it by the mane, strike it down, and kill it. I've killed lions and bears. And that uncircumcised Philistine will end up just like them for challenging the army of the Living God. God, who saved me from lion and bear, will save me from that Philistine."

"Then go," said Saul. "And may God be with you."

Saul gave David his own uniform. He put a bronze helmet and armor on him, as well as a sword. But David was not used to them and couldn't walk. So he took off the entire armor. He took his stick, and he picked up a few smooth stones from the riverbed and put them in his pocket. With sling in hand, he went toward the Philistine....

David said to the Philistine, "You come against me with sword, spear, and javelin.

I come against you in the name of *Adonai Tz'vaot,* God of Israel, whom you have defied...."

David put his hand in his bag, took out a stone, and slung it from his sling. The stone hit the Philistine between the eyes and sank into his forehead. He fell flat on his face. And so, David beat the Philistine with sling and stone. He struck him down and killed him without a sword. Then David ran up and stood over the Philistine. He took the Philistine's sword from its sheath and cut off his head.

I SAMUEL 17:32–40, 45, 49–51

## Saul Becomes Jealous

David's defeat of Goliath was a great success for the people of Israel against the Philistines. But it created a new problem. Suddenly David was a bigger hero than Saul.

When the troops came home and David returned from killing the Philistine, the women of all the Israelite towns began singing:

*"Saul killed thousands,*
*David has killed tens of thousands!"*

Saul was very upset when he heard this. He said, "They are saying David killed ten times as many as I did. He is trying to take my throne from me!" From that day on, Saul kept a jealous eye on David....

Saul asked his son Jonathan and his friends to kill David. But Jonathan and David were good friends. Jonathan told David, "My father is determined to kill you. Be on your guard tomorrow morning. Find a good hiding place and stay there. I'll go try to talk to my father."

Jonathan went to his father and said, "Please don't be angry with David. He's done nothing wrong to you. Everything he's done has been to help you. He took his own life in his hands when he killed the Philistine. God gave us a great victory that day. You saw and were happy. So why would you want to kill David, an innocent man?"

Saul listened to Jonathan and said, "By God, you're right. I won't put him to death."

I SAMUEL 18:6–9; 19:1–6

Saul's change of heart didn't last. He again became suspicious of David and was determined to see him dead. Whenever he wasn't battling the Philistines, Saul was trying to track down and kill David.

After a battle with the Philistines, Saul found out that David was staying in the desert of En-Gedi. So Saul took an army of three thousand men and went in search of David. He came to a hillside where sheep grazed. Saul found a cave where he could go to the bathroom. He didn't know that it was the very place where David was hiding.

While Saul was urinating, David sneaked up and quietly cut off the corner of Saul's coat. Afterward he felt very bad for cutting the coat. He said, "God forbid I should do that to God's anointed. I shouldn't raise my hand against him, because he is God's anointed."

Saul left the cave and started on his way. Then David came out and called to him, "Your Majesty the King! You shouldn't think that I am out to hurt you. Don't you see that God gave me the chance to kill you in this cave today? I could have killed you, but I cannot hurt God's anointed. Please, sir, take a look at this corner of fabric I hold in my hand. I cut it from your coat when I just as easily could have killed you. Don't you see that I have no intention of hurting you? You are determined to take my life. May God be a judge between us, but my hand will never touch you...."

When David finished speaking, Saul broke down and wept.

I SAMUEL 24:2–13, 17

As the Book of **First Samuel** ends, Saul suffered the saddest tragedy of his life. The Philistines attacked the Israelites at Mount Gilboa, and three of Saul's sons—including Jonathan—were killed. With the battle still waging, Saul looked down on the corpses of his sons, and then up at the attacking Philistine army, and announced that he wouldn't let the Philistines kill him. Instead he fell on his own sword and died.

Judaism teaches that suicide is a tragic and terrible sin. When a person takes his or her own life, they not only hurt themselves, but they hurt everyone who loves them, including God.

Why do you think Judaism teaches that suicide is a sin against God? Summarize your answer below.

_____

_____

_____

_____

King Saul's pain and sadness had to have been very strong for him to commit suicide. What thoughts do you think were going through Saul's mind when he fell on his own sword? What do you think were Saul's biggest regrets in life?

_____

_____

_____

_____

*Saul was the first king of Israel. But he was not Israel's greatest king. When, as the Bible tells us, Saul disappointed God, a new king was chosen. That was to be David, the greatest king of Israel. After seven years of rivalry between David and Saul's last surviving son, David would emerge as the king of all Israel, as we shall read in the next chapter.*

# Chapter Nine

## DAVID: KING OF ISRAEL

*After years on the run from Saul, David was now able to come out of hiding and take his place as the greatest king in Israel's history. In this chapter, we will read about King David's triumphs and his failings.*

After the death of Saul, it was time for David to reunite the tribes of Israel. His first step was to come out of hiding and present himself to the Israelites as their king.

Some time later, David asked God, "Should I visit one of the towns of Judah?"

God answered, "Yes."

Then David asked, "Which town should I go to?"

"To Hebron," answered God.

So David went to Hebron, along with his two wives and the families that were traveling with him.

Then the people of Judah came out and anointed David as king over the House of Judah.

II SAMUEL 2:1–4

Accepted as the king of Judah, David now needed to be accepted as king of the remaining tribes. That task wasn't so easy, since the northern tribes had long-standing allegiance with Saul and believed that one of his descendants should be king.

The war between the House of Saul and the House of David was long and drawn out. But David kept growing stronger, while the House of Saul grew weaker. While living in Hebron, David had several children. His first son was Amnon. His second was Chileab. His third was Absalom. The fourth was Adonijah, followed by Shephatiah and Ithream.

II SAMUEL 3:1–5

# Israel United

While in Hebron, David was eventually able to bring the two sides together again. He united Judah with the tribes of Israel and was able to put aside the differences between him and the House of Saul—for the time being.

While the northern tribes accepted David, they never completely accepted control by the tribe of Judah. To them, Judah was like a bossy older brother or sister, telling them what to do and where to pray.

Do you have an older brother or sister? Perhaps you are an older brother or sister. What sort of thing do brothers and sister argue about?

_____

_____

What kinds of problems can occur when one sister or brother sets down rules for the other brothers and sisters?

_____

_____

_____

Despite these conflicts, it was in the best interest of the northern tribes to accept and anoint David. He strengthened the entire Israelite nation.

Hebron had always been the capital city of Judah. David decided that a compromise was needed to help make the northern tribes feel that they weren't merely slaves to the tribe of Judah. To do this, he decided to move the capital of the Israelite nation to a neutral location.

The city of Jerusalem didn't belong to any of the Israelite tribes. It belonged to a people called the Jebusites. It was a beautiful and well-situated city that sat just north of the Judean border. The center of Jerusalem sat on a hill known as Zion.

The Bible tells us very little about the conquest of Jerusalem. David and his armies went into the city and were told that even the blind and disabled Jebusites could defeat them.

We are not told whether the conquest of Jerusalem was peaceful or violent. The Bible records insults about the blind and the disabled, but nothing about fighting or military resistance. Were the Jebusite people unhappy about the arrival of the Israelites? Or did they willingly welcome them and accept their ways? All that we know for certain is that David and the Israelites entered Jerusalem and Zion became his throne.

All the tribes of Israel came to David at Hebron and said, "We are part of your family. Back when Saul was our king, you were our greatest war hero. God asked you to shepherd Israel, to be its ruler.

The elders of Israel met with David and made an agreement before God. They anointed David king over Israel.

David was thirty years old when he became king, and he reigned for forty years. He ruled from Hebron for six and a half years. Then in Jerusalem he ruled for thirty-three years.

When King David and his men set out

toward Jerusalem, to battle the Jebusites who were living there, people told him that he would never succeed, that even the blind and disabled of the Jebusites could hold them back. They didn't think he would get Jerusalem from the Jebusites. But David took the hill of Zion.

Zion became his base, and he renamed it "the city of David." David built fortifying walls around the whole area. David kept getting stronger, for God was with him.

King Hiram of Tyre sent cedar logs, builders, and stoneworkers to build a palace for David. David now truly felt that God had made him a great king over Israel.

David took more wives in Jerusalem. He had many more children: Shammua, Shobab, Nathan, Solomon, Ibhar, Elishua, Nepheg, Japhia, Elishama, Eliada, and Eliphelet.

II SAMUEL 5:1–16

Settled in Jerusalem, David built up the city and his palace. Then he decided it was time to build a national sanctuary for God. It was time for a permanent Temple, he thought. But that wouldn't be the case.

Once the king had settled into his palace and God had granted him safety from hostile neighbors, he met with the prophet Nathan.

He told the prophet, "Here I am, sitting in a house of cedar, while the Ark of God is kept in a tent."

Nathan told the king to do whatever he thought was best, because God was with the king. But later that night, God spoke to Nathan and said, "Go tell my servant David: This is what God says: 'Are you the right person to build a house for me? From the time I brought the people out of Egypt I have not lived in a house. I have moved about in Tent and portable sanctuary. As I moved wherever the Israelites went, did I ever get angry with the Israelite leaders for not building me a house of cedar?'"

II SAMUEL 7:1–7

God's response to David seems strange. The king offered to build a house for God, and God didn't want it. What reason is given in the text?

_____

_____

_____

Later tradition teaches us that God did not want David to build the Temple because David was a man of war. David's son, Solomon, being a man of peace, was to be the one to build the House of God.

## "Ko Amar Adonai"

Nathan the prophet probably wasn't the first, but he was one of the earliest of the prophets to say *"Ko amar Adonai"* כֹּה אָמַר יְהוָה. The phrase means "God said this" or "this is what God said." Older Bible translations say, "Thus saith the Lord."

We find this phrase frequently when a prophet is speaking. It serves as an indication that in the lines that follow are the words spoken to the prophet by God.

## Bathsheba

The writers of the Bible were never shy about pointing out that their heroes weren't perfect. As great as King David was—as a king, as a soldier, and as a writer—he was human. He made mistakes and did some things that were very wrong. David was not above God's law. The Bible tells us about many incidents when God became angry with David. Even a king can be punished. This next story is one of the best examples of this.

David violated two of the Ten Commandments: "You shall not covet your neighbor's wife" and "You shall not commit adultery." He fell in love with a woman who was already married. The husband, a soldier in David's army, was away at battle.

Late one afternoon, David got up from his couch and strolled on the roof of the royal palace. There, from the roof, he saw a woman bathing. She was very beautiful. The king sent someone to find out about the woman. He learned that she was Bathsheba daughter of Eliam and wife of Uriah the Hittite. David summoned the woman. She came and they slept together, and then she returned to her home. When she discovered that she was pregnant, she told David.

David summoned Uriah the Hittite. He asked him about the troops and the war and then told him to take the night off, go home, and spend the night with his wife.

The next morning, David learned that Uriah hadn't listened to him, but had gone back with the other officers and spent the night at the palace entrance. David asked him, "Why didn't you go to your house?"

Uriah answered, "The Ark and Israel and Judah are in tents. My captain, Joab, and the rest of your army are camping out in the open. How do you expect me to go home, eat, drink, and sleep with my wife? Don't ask me to do it."

David said, "Stay another day, and then return to your duties."

David fed him and got him drunk. Again Uriah didn't go home. He slept in the same place with the other officers.

In the morning, David wrote a letter for Uriah to deliver to Joab, which instructed Joab to place Uriah in the front line of battle where the fighting is the fiercest, so that Uriah might be killed. When Joab led a battle against a city, he stationed Uriah in the front, and when they were attacked, Uriah was among the officers who died....

When Uriah's wife found out that her husband had been killed, she sorrowed over her husband. When the period of mourning was over, David sent for her. They were married and had a son.

But God was not happy with what David had done. God sent Nathan to David. Nathan said to him, "Two men were living in a town. One was rich and the other was poor. The rich man had large flocks and herds, but the poor man had only one little lamb that he had bought. That lamb was a part of his family. The rich man needed a lamb to make a meal for a guest, but he didn't want to use any of his own flock, so he took the poor man's lamb and served it to his guest."

David flew into a rage. He said to Nathan, "By God, the man who did that ought to die! He shall pay four times the cost of that lamb because he of what he did, showing no pity."

Nathan said, "You are that man. The God of Israel says, 'I anointed you king over Israel. I rescued you from Saul. I gave you the House of Israel and the House of Judah. I would have given you all you needed. Why have you done something so displeasing to Me? You put Uriah the Hittite to the sword and stole his wife. Therefore, the sword shall never depart from your house!"

II SAMUEL 11:2–17, 26–27; 12:1–10

The above text tells us of a terrible thing that Kind David did. What did he do that was wrong? See how many sins you can list that David committed:

_____

_____

_____

The prophet Nathan told David an important story-lesson. What did his story have to do with David's crimes? In the spaces below, describe Nathan's story and its relationship to David.

| NATHAN'S STORY | DAVID'S SINS |
|---|---|
| _____ | _____ |
| _____ | _____ |
| _____ | _____ |
| _____ | _____ |
| _____ | _____ |
| _____ | _____ |
| _____ | _____ |
| _____ | _____ |
| _____ | _____ |
| _____ | _____ |
| _____ | _____ |

God never let David forget the sin he had committed. The son of David and Bathsheba (the Bible never tells his name) became very ill and soon died. David regretted what he had done. Soon David and Bathsheba had another son. He was named Solomon, and he would be the last king of a united Israel.

# Absalom

At this point, the bravest and strongest of King David's children was his third son, Absalom. He would have made an ideal king, but a terrible fight between Absalom and his father drove them apart. David's eldest son, Amnon, was in love with his half-sister Tamar, and he tried to sleep with her. He forced her against her will, and understandably upset, she went to her other brother, Absalom, for protection. Absalom was so angry with his older brother that he had him killed. Despite the bad thing Amnon had done, King David was furious at Absalom for killing Amnon. Absalom ran away.

In addition to being angry with Absalom, King David was probably sad and disappointed with his son. What do you think David wanted to say to Absalom after he learned of the death of Amnon?

_____

_____

As war grew between David and Absalom, David tried to reconcile with Absalom. Absalom pretended to do the same. Actually, though, he was preparing to overthrow David by raising his own army of rebels. At first Absalom was successful. But David rallied and gained the upper hand. Nonetheless, he ordered his troops to spare Absalom's life. Sadly, the king's own officers spotted Absalom and killed him. David was very nervous throughout the battle and kept asking his messengers if Absalom was all right. Eventually he got word of Absalom's death.

The king was shaken. He went to the upper chamber of the gateway and wept, crying these words as he went:

"My son Absalom, my son, my son Absalom. If only I had died instead of you! Oh Absalom, my son, my son!"

II SAMUEL 19:1

# The End of David's Life

David was far from perfect. He had many moral weaknesses. His first six sons were all born of different mothers. His first wife was Michal, the daughter of Saul. Even though she once saved his life, Michal and David never had a good relationship, and she never had any children.

And yet, David is still considered the greatest king who ever ruled over Israel. The six-pointed star that much later became a symbol of Judaism is called *Magen David*, "the Star of David." One of the first songs a child learns in religious school is "David Melech Yisrael." The prophets of the Bible said that the messiah would come from the seed of David (from David's descendants) and would reestablish the kingdom of David.

**What do you think made David a "great" king? Why has he become such an important figure?**

_____

_____

As our final text for this chapter, we say goodbye to King David:

When David's life was drawing to a close, he gave the following instructions to his son Solomon: "I am going the way of all the earth. Be strong and act like a man. Follow God's instructions, walk in God's ways. Follow God's rules, mitzvot, and judgments as recorded in the Torah of Moses so that you may succeed in whatever you do. God has promised me that if my descendants are good and follow God faithfully with their heart and soul, then the throne of Israel under our dynasty will never end....

David slept with his fathers. He was buried in the city of David. He reigned over Israel for forty years. For seven years he ruled in Hebron, and for thirty-three years he ruled in Jerusalem.

Solomon sat on the throne of his father David, and his rule was firmly established.

I KINGS 2:1–4, 10–12

*Next, we will get to know Solomon, the son of David. While David is remembered for uniting the tribes of Israel and making Jerusalem its capital, Solomon would be best remembered for his wisdom, his love, and his construction of the Temple in Jerusalem.*

# Chapter Ten

## KING SOLOMON AND THE TEMPLE IN JERUSALEM

*After King David, the best remembered king of Israel was his son, Solomon. The reign of King Solomon is recorded in the first eleven chapters of **First Kings**. Like the two kings who ruled before him, Solomon's kingship had its difficulties. In this chapter, we will get to know Solomon and the Temple he built for God.*

If one word could characterize Solomon, the son of David and Bathsheba, it is "planning." King David was impulsive—quick to jump into situations that he might later regret. Solomon—wise King Solomon—was never impulsive. He never lost his temper, never jumped the gun, but always had strategies in mind, planning his next step.

As careful as Solomon tried to be though, his planning didn't always keep the best interests of God in mind. In order to extend his control throughout the Middle East, Solomon married the daughters of many foreign kings. Instead of teaching them the religion of Israel and the worship of one God, Solomon allowed his wives—and everyone else for that matter—to worship any and every god they chose. This, the Bible writers tell us, made God very unhappy.

Why do you think God might have been angry with Solomon?

_____

_____

In the beginning of his reign, Solomon had the favor of God, and God gave him deep wisdom, as we learn from the following text:

Solomon allied with Pharaoh, the king of Egypt, by marrying his daughter. He brought her to the City of David while he was finishing work on his palace, on the House of God, and on the walls around Jerusalem.

The people continued to offer sacrifices in the various shrines, because at that time the Temple had not yet been built. Solomon loved God and followed the practices of his father David, but he also made sacrifices at the shrines.

The king went to Gibeon, where there was the largest shrine, and made sacrifices there. While at Gibeon, God appeared to Solomon in a dream at night. God said, "What can I give you?"

Solomon said, "You were so kind to my father David, because he followed You faithfully with a whole heart. You continued your kindness by giving him a son to be king. Now you have made me king. I am still very young, with no leadership experience, and I find myself leading Your people, too numerous to count. Please, then, give me an understanding mind to judge between good and bad.

God was pleased with what Solomon had requested. God said, "You did not ask for a long life, you did not ask for riches, you did not ask that your enemies be killed. You asked for the ability to know justice. I now grant you a wise and judicious mind. There has never been anyone like you, and there never will be again. I shall also give you those things you didn't ask for: wealth and glory like no king has ever had. I will grant you a long life if you walk in My ways and observe My Torah and mitzvot, as your father David did.

Solomon awoke and realized it was a dream. He went to Jerusalem and stood before the Ark of the Covenant of God, sacrificed burnt offerings, and made a banquet.

Later, two women came to the king. The first woman said, "Please, your majesty, she and I live in the same house. We had babies three days apart. Then one night, her baby died. She got up in the night and switched my baby with her dead one. When I arose to feed my son I saw that he was dead. But when I looked closely I saw that it was not my son."

The other woman spoke up, "No, the live one is my son, and the dead one is yours."

But the first one said, "No, the dead one is yours, and the live one is mine."

They went on arguing like this before the king.

The king said, "You say the live one is yours. And you say the live one is yours. Fetch me a sword. We shall cut the baby in two and give one half to you and the other half to you."

But one of the women pleaded, "Please, your majesty, let her have the live child. Just don't kill him!"

The other woman said, "Neither of us should have him. Cut him in two!"

Then the king spoke: "This one shall have the child. She is the true mother."

I KINGS 3:1–27

In Solomon's dream, God offered Solomon one gift. What gift did Solomon choose?

_____

_____

Because of Solomon's wisdom, later Bible writers would credit him with writing two of the widsom books: **Proverbs** and **Ecclesiastes.** We will be looking at both of these books later.

# Solomon's Temple

The First Temple built in Jerusalem is often called "Solomon's Temple," and the Bible says repeatedly that Solomon built the Temple. In truth, Solomon probably never picked up a hammer or shovel during this or any other construction. When we say "Solomon built" the Temple, we really mean that "Solomon supervised the building" of the Temple. It was under Solomon's orders that it was built, and it was during his reign that it was begun and completed.

Solomon hired great craftsmen from all over the Middle East. He purchased stones, fabric, and metal from near and far. Where did the money come from for this major construction project? The money came from the people of Israel. Just as governments do today, King Solomon raised taxes.

More than fifty years earlier, Samuel had warned the people that this would happen. He said that a king would tax the people, taking their best things and demanding higher and higher percentages of their produce. With all of Solomon's great successes, it is important to keep in mind that the people didn't like being taxed. The high tax rate was one of the reasons the northern tribes would break away after Solomon's death.

Before we read the actual text of the construction of the Temple, we should go over a few things about the sanctuary customs of the ancient Israelites.

In Hebrew, several words are used for Temple: *Bayit* בַּיִת (House), *Heichal* הֵיכָל (Palace), and *Mikdash* מִקְדָּשׁ (Sanctuary). The Temple of Solomon would have a similar design to the Tent of Meeting (*Ohel Mo-eid* אֹהֶל מוֹעֵד) or the portable sanctuary (*Mishkan* מִשְׁכָּן) that the Israelites had used in the desert, according to the books of the Torah.

The common measurement at the time was the cubit (*amah* אַמָּה in Hebrew), which was the distance from an average man's elbow to his fingertips—about eighteen inches. With that in mind, the inside of the Temple was about the size of a basketball court.

The inside of the Temple was divided into several large halls, or chambers. The innermost chamber was called the Holy of Holies. It was a room about thirty feet long, thirty feet wide, and thirty feet high. It had the floor space of a typical classroom. The Holy of Holies had only one entrance, and inside were kept the Ark of the Covenant and two statues of winged creatures called *k'ruvim* כְּרוּבִים in Hebrew (most Bibles spell it "cherubim"). These mythical creatures were believed to be among God's helpers and were the guards at the Garden of Eden.

What made the Holy of Holies special? According the Rabbis of the Talmud, the Holy of Holies was the innermost dwelling of God. It was there that God's Presence rested. The Ark of the Covenant in the Holy of Holies was God's throne.

Below is a folktale, told by the Yiddish writer S. Ansky in his play *The Dybbuk*. This story is told by Rabbi Azrielke as part of his sermon:

God's world is great and holy.
Among the holy lands in the world is the
Holy Land of Israel.
In the Land of Israel, the holiest city is
Jerusalem.
In Jerusalem, the holiest place was the
Temple.
In the Temple, the holiest place was the
Holy of Holies.

There are seventy nations in the world.
Among these holy nations is the People of
Israel.
The holiest of the people of Israel is the
tribe of Levi.
In the tribe of Levi, the holiest are the
priests.
Among the priests, the holiest was the
High Priest.

There are 354 days in a (Hebrew) year.

Among these days, the festivals are holy.
Higher than these is the holiness of
Shabbat.
Among Shabbatot, the holiest is Yom
Kippur, the Sabbath of Sabbaths.

There are seventy languages in the world.
Among the holy languages is the holy
language of Hebrew.
Holier than all else in this language is the
holy Torah.
In the Torah, the holiest part is the Ten
Commandments.
In the Ten Commandments, the holiest of
all words is the Name of God.

Once during the year, at a certain hour, these four supreme sanctities of the world were joined with one another. That was on the Day of Atonement when the High Priest would enter the Holy of

Holies and there would utter the Name of God. And because this hour was infinitely holy and awesome, it was the time of utmost peril not only for the High Priest, but for all Israel. God forbid if, in this hour, a false or sinful thought were to enter the mind of the High Priest, the entire world would have been destroyed.

*Wherever a man raises his eyes to heaven is a Holy of Holies.*

*Every person, having been created in the image and likeness of God, is a High Priest.*

*Every day of a person's life is a Day of Atonement.*

*Every word that a person breathes is the name of God.*

S. ANSKY, *THE DYBBUK*

According to Rabbi Azrielke's story, what makes the Holy of Holies a special place? What happens in it?

_____

_____

_____

This text describes the construction of the "House of God" built under the reign of Solomon:

Four hundred and eighty years after the Israelites left the land of Egypt, Solomon began to build the House of God. The House that King Solomon built for God was sixty cubits long, twenty cubits wide, and thirty cubits high. The entryway in front of the Great Hall was twenty cubits long, running along the width of the House, and ten cubits deep in front of the House. There were windows set in with lattices. There was a multistoried structure with side chambers all around. The bottom floor was five cubits wide, the middle one six cubits wide, and the third seven cubits wide.

When the House was built, all that was used were finished stones that had been precut at the quarry. No hammer or ax or iron tool was heard in the House while it was being built....

The word of God came to Solomon, "Regarding the House that you are building, if you follow My Torah and observe My rules and faithfully keep My mitzvot, I will keep the promise I made with your father David. I will stay with the Children of Israel and will never forsake them."

When Solomon finished construction of the House, he paneled the walls with planks of cedar. He covered the floor in cypress. Twenty cubits from the rear of the House he set up a separate room with cedar planks that went from the floor to the rafters. He furnished this room as the Shrine.… It was the Holy of Holies. This innermost room was the place for the Ark of God's Covenant. Inside the Shrine was twenty cubits wide, twenty cubits long, and twenty cubits high. He had it overlaid in solid gold. He also overlaid the cedar altar. Solomon overlaid the inside of the House with solid gold and put gold chains in the door of the Shrine. The entire House was overlaid with gold when it was completed.

Inside the Shrine he made two olive wood cherubim, each ten cubits high. The wings of each were five cubits long, giving them a wingspan of ten cubits. Both cherubim were exactly the same size and design.

He put the cherubim inside the Shrine, so that the wings stretched across to each other and to the opposite walls. Both cherubim were overlaid in gold.

I KINGS 6:1–7, 11–16, 19–28

## Solomon the Lover

Solomon was also known for being a man who loved women. The Bible tells us that he had 700 wives of full status as well as 300 concubines, wives of lower status—numbers that many find hard to believe.

Among the later books in the Bible is a collection of love poetry called **Song of Songs.** No one knows for certain who wrote this book. Even though it was probably written long after Solomon's death, the author wrote it as though it were by King Solomon.

The many loves of Solomon drew God's anger, as we learn from the following text:

King Solomon loved many foreign women. In addition to the Pharaoh's daughter, there were Moabite, Ammonite, Edomite, Phoenician, and Hittite women. They were from all the nations that God had told the Israelites not to mix with lest they follow their gods. King Solomon had 700 wives and 300 concubines. These women turned Solomon's heart astray. He was no longer as completely devoted to God as his father David had been. Solomon followed Ashtoreth, the goddess of the Phoenicians, and Milcom, the idol of the Ammonites....

God was angry with Solomon because he had gone astray from the God of Israel, who had appeared to him twice. So God told Solomon, "Because you are guilty of this, of not keeping my Covenant and the Torah which I gave you, I will tear the kingdom away from you and give it to one of your servants. In memory of your father, David, I will not tear it away while you are alive. I will tear it away from your son, leaving him but one tribe, in memory of David and for the sake of Jerusalem.

I KINGS 11:1–5, 9–13

Why was God angry with Solomon?

_____

_____

What punishment did God promise Solomon because of his actions?

_____

_____

The punishment might have been much harsher. Why was Solomon's punishment as light as it was?

_____

_____

# Jeroboam and Rehoboam: The Splitting of the People

Jeroboam was a young man from the tribe of Ephraim who worked as one of Solomon's construction foremen. The Bible doesn't tell us much more about him, until he became the leader of a rebellion against the king that would lead to a civil war.

The guiding light behind the rebellion was a prophet named Ahijah, from the northern city of Shiloh.

Jeroboam's rival was King Solomon's son, Rehoboam. After the death of King Solomon, these two men with similar-sounding names would rule the two separate Israelite kingdoms.

While Jeroboam was leaving Jerusalem, he met the prophet Ahijah of Shiloh. When the two of them were alone in the open country, Ahijah took the new robe that Jeroboam was wearing and tore it into twelve pieces.

He told Jeroboam, "You take ten pieces. For God has said, 'I will tear the kingdom from Solomon's hands. I give you ten tribes, and he will keep one, for the sake of David and Jerusalem....'"

Solomon now wanted Jeroboam dead. But Jeroboam fled to King Shishak of Egypt and remained in Egypt until Solomon died.

The rest of the events of Solomon's reign, all his actions and his wisdom, are written in the records of Solomon. Solomon reigned in Jerusalem over all Israel for forty years. He slept with his fathers and was buried in the city of his father, David. His son Rehoboam suceeded him as king.

I KINGS 11:29–32, 40–43

*In this chapter, we learned about the reign of King Solomon and his building of the Temple. With the rebellion of Jeroboam, the stage has been set for the great civil war that would divide Israel into two nations. In the next chapter, we will learn how those two kingdoms would manage over the next two hundred years and about the trials and sins of their many kings.*

# Chapter Eleven

# THE TWO KINGDOMS

It was always very difficult for the twelve tribes of Israel to stay together as a single kingdom. After the death of King Solomon, the northern tribes rebelled against Judah and set up their own nation, the Kingdom of Israel. In this chapter, we will read about the kings and prophets of Judah and Israel, and about one prophet in particular: Elijah of Tishbi.

After the death of Solomon, his son Rehoboam became the new king of Judah. But the rest of Israel had not accepted him as their king. He went to Shechem, where the leaders of the other tribes were meeting. He asked the leaders to anoint him as king over all the Israelite tribes.

But Jeroboam, together with the prophet Ahijah, encouraged the people **not** to accept Rehoboam's offer. They said:

*"We have no investment in David,*
*We have no share in Jesse's son.*
*To your tents, Israel!*
*You keep to yourselves, David."*

So the Israelites returned to their homes. But Rehoboam continued to reign over the people who lived in the territory of Judah.

King Rehoboam sent Adoram, who was in charge of the labor, but the Israelites pelted him to death with stones. So King Rehoboam quickly got on his chariot and rushed to Jerusalem. That is how Israel revolted against the House of David.

When all Israel heard that Jeroboam had returned, they sent messengers and summoned him to the assembly and made him king over all Israel. Only the tribe of Judah remained loyal to the House of David.

When Rehoboam returned to Jerusalem, he gathered an army from the tribes of Judah and Benjamin, an army of 180,000 top soldiers to fight against the House of Israel in order to restore the kingship to Rehoboam son of Solomon.

But the word of God came to a man of God named Shemaiah, "Tell Rehoboam son of Solomon—king of Judah and Benjamin—do not make war against your cousins the Israelites. Everyone should return home. This is all part of My plan."

The people followed the word of God and turned back as God had said.

I KINGS 12:16–24

And so there was a split in the kingdom. North and south separated just as the American states separated in 1861. The two kingdoms—Israel to the north and Judah to the south—each had their own king and their own holy places.

Can you think of any other times when a nation, a club, or any other group split up because of a disagreement?

_____

_____

| The Kings of Judah and Israel (B.C.E.) | |
| --- | --- |
| **Judah** | **Israel** |
| Saul (1028–1013) | |
| David (1013–1006) * | Saul (1013–1006) * |
| David (1006–973) | |
| Solomon (973–933) | |
| Rehoboam (933–917) | Jeroboam (933–912) |
| Abijam (917–915) | Nadab (912–911) |
| Asa (915–875) | Baasha (911–888) |
| | Elah (888–887) |
| | Zimri (887) |
| | Omri (887–875) |
| Jehoshaphat (875–851) | Ahab (875–853) |
| Jehoram (851–844) | Ahaziah (853–852) |
| Ahaziah (844–843) | Jehoram (852–843) |
| Athaliah (843–837) | Jehu (843–816) |
| Jehoash (837–797) | Jehoahaz (816–800) |
| Amaziah (797–780) | Joash (800–785) |
| Uzziah/Azariah (780–740) | Jeroboam II (785–738) |
| Jotham (740–736) | Zechariah (738–737) |
| Ahaz (736–720) | Shallum (737) |
| Hezekiah (720–693) | Menahem (737) |
| Manasseh (693–642) | Pekahiah (738–737) |
| Amon (642–638) | Pekah (737–732) |
| Josiah (638–609) | Hoshea (732–722) |
| Jehoahaz (609–608) | **Fall of Israel to Assyria (722)** |
| Jehoiakim (608–598) | |
| Jehoiachin (598–597) | |
| Zedekiah (597–586) | |
| **Babylonian exile (586)** | |

* During the seven-year period 1013–1006 B.C.E., Saul and David were both kings of the separate nations.

One of the differences between the Northern Kingdom and the Southern Kingdom is the way—and the place—they worshiped God. The people of Israel brought their offerings to various altars and sanctuaries like those at Shiloh, Bethel, and Shechem. In Judah, the people believed that there was only one place to make offerings to God: at the Temple built by Solomon in Jerusalem.

From 933 B.C.E. (when King Solomon died) until 722 B.C.E., there was a long succession of kings in both the north and south.

The stories of the kings of the Northern Kingdom and the Southern Kingdom are told through the rest of the Books of **First** and **Second Kings**. These stories skip back and forth between north and south. Some of the kings were very good. But most of them, the text tells us, at some time during their rule did something that displeased God.

The person who wrote **Samuel** and **Kings** was from the Southern Kingdom of Judah. The writer didn't like the Northern Kingdom of Israel and believed that God was angry with it. Why do you think the writer described it that way? Do you think God really was angry with the Northern Kingdom?

_____

_____

The writer tells us that King Asa of Judah, the fourth king after David, was a very good king. All of the kings of Israel, the writer tells us, constantly did things to anger God.

In this next text, we will read about some of the northern kings:

In the thirty-first year of King Asa of Judah, Omri became king over Israel and ruled for twelve years. He ruled in Tirzah for six of the years and then built a capital in Samaria. Omri did what was displeasing to God. He was worse than all who ruled before him. He was like Jeroboam, committing the same sins and causing Israel to commit sins. The rest of his activities and all the things he did are written in the records of the kings of Israel. Omri slept with his father and was buried in Samaria. His son Ahab succeeded him as king.

Ahab son of Omri became king of Israel in the thirty-eighth year of King Asa of Judah. Ahab reigned in Samaria for twenty-two years. Ahab did what was displeasing to God, worse than any who ruled before him. He committed sins far worse than the sins that Jeroboam committed. He married a Phoenician princess, Jezebel daughter of Ethbaal. Ahab began to worship the god Baal. He set up an altar to Baal in a temple that he built in Samaria for Baal. Ahab also made a sacred pole. He did more to anger God than all the kings of Israel who were before him did.

I KINGS 16:23–33

Ahab, the son of Omri, would become one of the most important—and most notorious—of the northern kings. He and his wife, Jezebel, did more to anger the prophets and priests of Judah than any other Israelite.

What do you think Ahab did that would displease God?

_____

_____

# Samaria

In the previous text, King Omri of Israel set up a new capital in the town of Samaria. Samaria became as important to the Northern Kingdom as Jerusalem was to the people of Judah. Before long the name "Samaria" was used to describe the entire Kingdom of Israel.

# Elijah of Tishbi

We meet Elijah the prophet, who would become a legend in his time and on to our own. Elijah (his name means "*Adonai* is my God") lived in the Northern Kingdom and spoke out against the worship of the ancient local gods Baal and Asherah. He demanded that the kings of Israel change their bad ways and return to the worship of God, and he warned them of punishment if they continued to anger God.

Elijah was also a miracle worker, as we learn from this next text and others that follow.

Elijah of Tishbi, who lived in Gilead, said to Ahab, "By the God of Israel, there will be no dew or rain until you do as I say."

The word of God came to Elijah, telling him, "Go off to the east and stay near Wadi Cherith. Drink from the wadi, and I will have the ravens bring you food there."

He did as God had said and stayed by Wadi Cherith, east of the Jordan. Every morning and evening ravens would bring him bread and meat.

Eventually the wadi dried up because there was a drought in the land. The word of God came to him and said, "Go now to Zarephath. You shall stay with a widow who will feed you."

So he went to Zarephath, and at the town entrance he met a widow collecting wood. "Could I please have a little water to drink?" he said to her. As she turned, he said, "Could I also have a piece of bread?"

"I swear to God I have nothing baked. All I have is a handful of flour in a jar and a bit of oil in a bottle. I am gathering sticks so that I can bake something for my son and me. When it's gone we shall die."

"Don't be afraid," Elijah told her. "Go and do just as you said. But first bake something for me. The God of Israel says that the flour will not run out, and the bottle of oil will not become empty until the day God sends rain."

The woman did as Elijah said. She and her son had plenty of food, for the flour never ran out, and the oil bottle was never empty.

Some time later the woman's son became sick. The illness became so bad that he stopped breathing. The woman asked Elijah, "Did I do something hurtful to you, O man of God, that you made my son die?"

"Give me your son," he said. And he took the body upstairs to his room and put it on his bed. He cried out to God, "*Adonai* my God, will You allow a tragedy to happen to the woman whose guest I am, letting her son die?" He stretched out over the boy three times and said, "*Adonai* my God, let the boy's life return to his body."

God heard Elijah's plea, and the boy revived. Elijah took him down to his mother and said, "Look, your son is alive."

And she answered, "Now I am sure that you are a man of God and that God's words really are in your mouth."

1 KINGS 17:1–24

In the above text, what sort of things did Elijah do that were miraculous?

_____

_____

_____

By this time, the prophets were more than a few odd spokesmen. There was an entire class of people, both in Judah and in Israel, who actively spoke against evil actions of the kings and idolatrous practices of the people.

Many people in Israel didn't want to hear what the prophets had to say. They worshiped the Baalim and Ashtaroth of the other nations, perhaps because they believed these gods would provide them with extra benefits, besides what they get from *Adonai*. Queen Jezebel, who was encouraging the people to worship her gods, was angry with the prophet class and tried to have all the prophets killed.

Elijah arranged a unique lesson for Ahab and the people. He called for a public meeting with Ahab and 450 prophets of Baal. He asked everyone, "How long will you continue to jump back and forth between two beliefs? If *Adonai* is God, then follow *Adonai*. If Baal is god, then follow him!" The prophets of Baal set up a fancy altar with a sacrifice, and they danced and chanted, cut up the animals, and called out to Baal. But nothing happened.

Then Elijah set up rocks around a broken altar and built an alter big enough to cook a bull offering. He told some people to pour water on the altar again and again, until it was soaked. Suddenly fire descended from the sky and consumed Elijah's altar and everything on it. The people were so shocked that they all returned to the belief in *Adonai* as the one God. Elijah had all the prophets of Baal killed, and then he told King Ahab to hurry home before he got wet.

**Why do you think Elijah would say that to King Ahab?**

_____

_____

During all this time, the land of Israel was still suffering the drought. There had been little rain, the farms were short of produce, and the people were hungry. But when Elijah said this to Ahab, the sky turned dark and the clouds burst with rain.

## A Still Small Voice

There are times when God's messages are loud and clear. We have stories in our tradition of God revealed in thunderous mountains, pillars of fire, and a splitting sea. Scholars and historians can't be sure whether these huge events really happened. If the Sea of Reeds was really split for the Israelites to pass through, did God cause it? Is there a natural, scientific explanation? Were events like this made up by the writers of the Bible to illustrate the greatness of God?

We **can** be certain that God speaks to people in much more quiet and subtle ways. It is important not to confuse God's "voice" with a human voice. God's "voice" can come to people in pictures, dreams, and feelings. When God "speaks," there may not be any actual words or even sounds.

**What do you think the expression "still, small voice" means? What does it mean to you personally?**

_____

_____

The story of Elijah teaches us an important lesson. God won't come to us in a grand, Hollywood special-effects event. We can only hear God if we listen quietly and patiently for God's Presence, as Elijah did in this next text.

Ahab and Jezebel wanted to see Elijah dead. They were tired of the way he criticized the things they did and the gods they worshiped. Elijah knew that they wanted to kill him, but he could not help but say what he knew God wanted him to say. Fearing for his life, Elijah ran to the Judean wilderness to hide. Depressed and alone, he called out to God, "This is enough. Take my life now, God. Let me die like my ancestors."

He hid in a cave and stayed the night there. Then the word of God came to him, "Why are you here, Elijah?... Come out and stand on the mountain before God."

Then God passed by. There was a great and mighty wind, splitting mountains and shattering rocks. But God was not in the wind. After the wind, there was an earthquake. But God was not in the earthquake. After the earthquake, there was fire. But God was not in the fire.

After the fire came a still, small voice.

When Elijah heard it, he pulled his coat up around his face and went out to stand at the cave's entrance.

A voice said, "Why are you here, Elijah?"

He answered, "I am moved by passion for God. The Israelites have forgotten Your covenant. They have torn down Your altars and killed Your prophets. I am the only one left, and they are about to kill me."

I KINGS 19:9, 11–14

All the prophets described their revelations—their meetings with God—in different ways. Match the prophet below with the moment of his revelation.

| | |
|---|---|
| Abraham | Ladder to heaven |
| Jacob | Burning bush |
| Moses | Samuel sleeping as child |
| Samuel | Akedah |

# Jezebel and the Theft of Naboth's Vineyard

King Ahab's wife, Jezebel, was considered such a wicked person that her name has become a symbol in the English language for a treacherous woman. It was once a common insult, when a woman did something especially mean and heartless, to call her a "Jezebel." The story of Naboth's vineyard describes her meanest deed.

Naboth of Jezreel owned a vineyard that was next to King Ahab's palace in Samaria. Ahab said to Naboth, "Let me have your vineyard. I want it for a vegetable garden, since it's right next to my palace. I'll trade you, giving you a better vineyard, or if you prefer I'll pay you in money."

But Naboth said, "I cannot give up what I inherited from my ancestors. God forbid!"

Ahab went home sorely disappointed at Naboth's response to his offer. He lay down on his bed and refused to eat. His wife Jezebel came to him and asked, "Why are you so depressed?"

He told her about his offer to Naboth and Naboth's response.

Jezebel told him, "It's time for you to act like a king. Get up and eat something. Be happy. I will get Naboth's vineyard for you."

So she wrote letters in Ahab's name to several leaders in Naboth's community. The letters told that there was to be a fast, followed by a trial of Naboth. Two crooked witnesses were to be hired to testify that Naboth had spoken against God and the king, and then Naboth was to be taken out and stoned to death....

As soon as Jezebel heard that Naboth had been stoned to death, she told Ahab, "Go and take the vineyard that Naboth of Jezreel refused to sell you. Naboth is now dead." And Ahab went out and took possession of the vineyard.

Then the word of God came to Elijah of Tishbi, "Go down and confront King Ahab of Israel who lives in Samaria. He is now in Naboth's vineyard, which he is taking possession of. Tell him, 'This is what God says: Would you murder a man and then become his heir? The very place where the dogs lapped up Naboth's blood, the dogs will lap up your blood as well.'"...

Regarding Jezebel, God said, "The dogs shall devour Jezebel in the field of Jezreel. All of Ahab's descendants who die in the city will be eaten by dogs, and all who die in the the open will be eaten by birds."

I KINGS 21:1–10, 15–19, 23–24

# Up in a Whirlwind

Have you ever wondered why Elijah the prophet is the invisible guest at every Passover seder? In part it is due to the story we are about to read. The Bible never tells us that Elijah died. Instead we learn that he was taken up to heaven in a whirlwind. This is the final passage about Elijah, in which he passed the responsibility on to his student, Elisha.

When God was about to take Elijah up to heaven in a whirlwind, Elijah and Elisha were on their way to Gilgal. Elijah said to Elisha, "Stay here. God wants me to go on to Bethel."

"By God and by your life," said Elisha, "I will not leave you."

So they went on to Jericho. The sons of the prophets in Jericho came over and said to Elisha, "Did you know that God is going to take your teacher away from you today?"

"I know," he said. "Be quiet."

Elijah told him, "Stay here. God wants me to go on to Jordan."

"By God and by your life," said Elisha, "I will not leave you." And the two of them continued on their way. They were followed by fifty of the sons of the prophets, who stood by at a distance when they stopped at the Jordan.

Elijah took off his coat and rolled it up. He struck the water, and it split to the right and the left so that they could cross the river dry. As they were crossing, Elijah said to Elisha, "Tell me, what can I do for you before I am taken from you?"

Elisha answered, "Let two-thirds of your spirit pass on to me."

"You have asked for something very difficult," he said. "If you watch me as I am being taken up, you will be granted your wish. If not, you will not."

They kept walking and talking, and then a fiery chariot with fiery horses suddenly appeared. The two men were separated, and Elijah went up to heaven in a whirlwind. Elisha saw it and cried out, "Father, father! Chariots and horsemen of Israel!" When the chariot was out of sight, Elisha grabbed his clothing and tore it in two.

He took Elijah's coat from where it had

been dropped, and he went back to the shore of the Jordan. Taking the rolled-up coat, he struck the water. It split to the sides, and he crossed over. When the sons of the prophets of Jericho saw him from a distance, they yelled, "The spirit of Elijah has settled on Elisha!" They ran to meet him and bowed to the ground.

II KINGS 2:1–15

What happened to Elijah? No one knows for sure. People's explanations have included angels, the hand of God, flying saucers, or a vivid imagination on the part of Elisha.

Do you have a theory of your own?

_____

_____

_____

The text tells us that two-thirds of Elijah's spirit passed on to Elisha. What do you think that means? How would Elisha be different now?

_____

_____

_____

Perhaps because of his mysterious disappearance, Elijah's spirit has remained a part of Jewish observance.

When a baby boy is circumcised, during a *b'rit milah,* the *sandak* who holds the baby sits in a chair called the *kisei Eliyahu*—the chair of Elijah.

At every Passover seder, we set a place at our tables and fill a glass of wine for our invisible guest, Elijah.

At the end of every Shabbat, after putting out the *Havdalah* candle, we sing the song, "Eliyahu HaNavi."

There are many Jewish folktales that feature Elijah. Often in folktales and legends, Elijah returns from heaven to visit people. In these stories, he generally provides help to the poor and rewards people for doing mitzvot. It is believed that Elijah will come to help welcome the Messiah at some future time.

Why do you think Elijah is such a popular character in Jewish folklore? What happened during his life that made him so memorable?

_____

_____

*The time of the divided kingdom was a time of many weak and sometimes wicked kings. It was also a time for the rise of prophets. Elijah and Elisha led the way as spokesmen for God, for right and wrong. In the next several chapters, we will be meeting more prophets and reading their own words condemning evil rulers and bad behavior.*

# Chapter Twelve

# THE LITERARY PROPHETS

*The Tanakh contains two very different kinds of prophetic books. So far, we have learned about the Historical Prophets, a set of books that tell the early history of the Israelite nation. In this chapter, we will learn about the Literary Prophets, books containing religious and political speeches written as poetry. As we read this chapter, pay close attention to the characteristics that make these books unique. In much of the rest of this book, we will be reading about the Literary Prophets.*

As we reach the middle chapter of this book, now is a good time to review the books of the *Tanakh* that we have studied so far.

## *Tanakh* Begins with Torah

The first five books of the *Tanakh* (Bible) are called *Torah* (Teaching) or *Chumash* (The Five). Sometimes people call these books by their Greek name, Pentateuch, which means "Five Vessels" or "Five Books."

| B'REISHIT | SH'MOT | VAYIKRA | B'MIDBAR | D'VARIM |
|---|---|---|---|---|
| בְּרֵאשִׁית | שְׁמוֹת | וַיִּקְרָא | בְּמִדְבַּר | דְּבָרִים |
| GENESIS | EXODUS | LEVITICUS | NUMBERS | DEUTERONOMY |

The five books of the Torah begin with the story of the Creation and tell of the beginnings of the Israelite people, their enslavement in Egypt, and their escape with Moses toward the land of Canaan.

In the space provided, list five stories or events that appear in the five books of the Torah.

1. _____

2. _____

3. _____

4. _____

5. _____

# Historical Prophets

The books of *N'vi-im* (Prophets) that we've studied so far are **Joshua**, **Judges**, **Samuel**, and **Kings**. They are often called the "Historical Prophets" because they tell of the history of the Israelite people after the death of Moses. They are also sometimes called the "Early Prophets" because they were written in and tell the stories of an earlier time than the other *N'vi-im* books.

# Literary Prophets

We now move on to that second group of prophetic books, which are often called the "Literary Prophets" or the "Later Prophets." You can think of the Literary Prophets as "Writing Prophets." All the prophets that we have encountered before—Samuel, Nathan, Elijah, and Elisha—were involved in the stories that we've read. The Books of **Joshua, Judges, Samuel,** and **Kings** told stories **about** these prophets. The Literary Prophets books were written **by** prophets. These books contain very few stories. They are a collection of sermons written in verse.

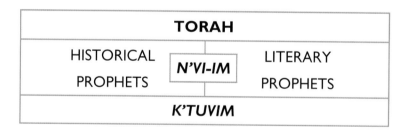

The Literary Prophets books are:

# Hebrew Verse

Nearly one-third of the Bible is written in poetry. In the popular JPS translation of the *Tanakh,* which is 1,624 pages long, a full 786 pages contain some poetry.

*Without some knowledge of Biblical poetry,*
*With no understanding of Hebrew verse,*
*We may as well be reading with our eyes half closed,*
*With our vision out of focus.*

So what is Hebrew verse? For our purposes, "verse" and "poetry" mean the same thing. In general, poetry makes use of elements that don't appear as frequently in everyday speech or even in other kinds of writings. The four lines above give you a good example of what Hebrew verse is like. We will go over the main elements: couplets, beats, mood, imagery, and parallelism. If these words are new to you, don't worry.

# Couplets and Beats

Nearly all poetry is made up of couplets and beats. A couplet is a set of two lines. Beats are the number of stressed syllables in a line. The beats set the rhythm of the poem. Another name for number of beats per line is "meter."

Look at this poem by William Blake. Blake was an English poet and printer who lived about two hundred years ago. He was a Christian who wrote his most famous works about God. Knowing that God couldn't be described directly, he used images from nature, in this case a tiger, to symbolize the wonder, power, and frightfulness of God. This is precisely what the prophets, psalmists, and sages had done two thousand years earlier.

### "The Tyger" by William Blake from Songs of Experience

1 Tyger Tyger, burning bright,
2 In the forests of the night;
3 What immortal hand or eye,
4 Could frame thy fearful symmetry?
5 In what distant deeps or skies.
6 Burnt the fire of thine eyes?
7 On what wings dare he aspire?
8 What the hand, dare seize the fire?

Look at lines 1 and 2 from the first couplet:

*Tyger Tyger, burning bright,*
*In the forests of the night;*

As you read those two lines aloud, listen for the rhythm. You may discover that each line has four beats (marked below in big bold letters):

***Ty**ger **Ty**ger, **bur**ning **bright**,*
***In** the **fo**rests **of** the **night**;*

In the Book of **Second Samuel**, when Saul and his son Jonathan died in battle, David recited the following lines from a longer poem:

| | |
|---|---|
| *Saul and Jonathan,* | שָׁאוּל וִיהוֹנָתָן |
| *Beloved and cherished* | הַנֶּאֱהָבִים וְהַנְּעִימִם |
| *In life and death,* | בְּחַיֵּיהֶם וּבְמוֹתָם |
| *Never apart.* | לֹא נִפְרָדוּ |
| *They were swifter than eagles,* | מִנְּשָׁרִים קַלּוּ |
| *They were stronger than lions.* | מֵאֲרָיוֹת גָּבֵרוּ |
| II SAMUEL 1:23 | |

The Hebrew has been provided to help you recognize the beats. You'll notice that in Hebrew, there are a lot of extra syllables between the beats. Hebrew poets weren't concerned with the exact number of syllables, as long as the number of beats, or stressed syllables, was even. This poem is made up of six lines. How many couplets are there?

The beats have been highlighted in bold print.

In the first couplet, each line has _____ beats.

In the second couplet, each line has _____ beats.

In the third couplet, each line has _____ beats.

You will find couplets and beats throughout the poetry in the Bible, as well as in nearly all poetry in every language and culture.

In English poetry, the ends of lines often rhyme (like the words "bright" and "night" in the poem by Blake). We don't find rhymes as often in Hebrew poetry.

And now on to the next characteristics of Hebrew verse…

# Mood and Image

Like couplets and beats, nearly all poems in every language and culture are filled with mood and image. By mood, we mean the emotion conveyed by a poem.

A common emotion we find in poems about God is the mood of awe. Awe is the feeling of amazement at how great something is. Standing atop a mountain, looking down at the world, we might be struck with awe. Visiting an animal reserve or zoo, we might feel awe looking face-to-face at an elephant, a panther, a gorilla, or a whale. Below is a sample of verse from the Book of **Psalms**:

*I know that God is great,*
*That our God is greater than all gods.*
*Whatever God wants, God does,*
*In heaven and earth*
*In the seas and the deep.*

*God makes clouds rise from the ends of*
*  the earth*
*God makes lightning for the rain*
*God lets loose wind from the heavens.*
                                    PSALM 135:5–7

Below are two more passages from the Book of **Psalms**. In the space provided below, write down the kind of emotion these words are trying to make you feel.

| | |
|---|---|
| *O God, do not punish me in anger,*<br>*Do not scold me in fury.*<br><br>*Have mercy on me, God, I am weak,*<br>*Heal me, God, my bones shake with fear.*<br><div align="right">PSALM 6:2–3</div> | *Sing on, righteous ones, to God!*<br><br><br>*It is good that the upright acclaim God.*<br>*Praise God with the lyre,*<br>*With the ten-stringed harp sing to God*<br>*Sing God a new song,*<br>*Play sweetly with shouts of joy!*<br><div align="right">PSALM 33:1–3</div> |
| What is the mood? | What is the mood? |

Imagery is the set of pictures that words create in our minds. With imagery, the poet tells us what something is like by showing us something else. In the example on page 113 from Psalm 135, we see the lines, "God makes lightning for the rain; God lets loose wind from the heavens." Reading those lines forces us to see lightning and rain, to hear wind and thunder, and this can help us feel God's power.

Some of the best imagery in the Bible is found in **Song of Songs.** In the following passage, a woman is describing the man she loves. It is easy to picture them in an apple grove and to taste crisp, dripping apples as they kiss:

*Like an apple tree among the forest trees,*
*That is my beloved among young men.*
*I delight to sit in his shade,*
*And his fruit is sweet to my mouth.*

SONG OF SONGS 2:3

Mood and image, like beats and couplets, are important in all poetry. The next characteristic is not as common in other languages and cultures, but is very important in Hebrew poetry.

# Parallelism

Parallelism is when words from one line in a couplet are paired up with words from the other line in that couplet. In the previous example, the phrase "an apple tree" is parallel to "my beloved," and "the forest trees" is parallel to "young men."

LIKE **AN APPLE TREE** AMONG **THE FOREST TREES**,

THAT IS **MY BELOVED** AMONG **YOUNG MEN**.

Notice how in this next example from Psalm 33, the parallel words are in a different order. This is called "crossed parallelism" or "chiasmus."

**PRAISE GOD** WITH THE **LYRE**,

WITH THE **TEN-STRINGED HARP SING** TO **GOD**

It's time to look again at the first piece of Bible poetry that we saw—King David's thoughts about King Saul and Saul's son Jonathan after they were killed in battle:

Saul and Jonathan,
Beloved and cherished
In life and death,

Never apart.
They were swifter than eagles,
They were stronger than lions.

II SAMUEL 1:23

- Use brackets { to mark the couplets.
- Place an accent mark > above words where you think the beat should be.
- Draw lines to connect any parallelisms you can find.
- What is the mood of the poem?

_____

_____

What images does the author provide to help us get a better picture of Saul and Jonathan?

_____

_____

# What Did the Prophets Say?

## A Timeline of the Literary Prophets

| | |
|---|---|
| 933 B.C.E. | **Death of King Solomon; the kingdom split into Israel and Judah** |
| 873–843 | Elijah active as a prophet |
| ~760 | Amos begins prophesying |
| ~750 | Hosea |
| ~740 | Isaiah |
| ~725 | Micah |
| 722 | **Israel destroyed by Assyria** |
| ~630 | Zephaniah |
| 626–586 | Jeremiah |
| ~615 | Nahum |
| 605 | Habakkuk |
| 597 | **First Babylonian exile** |
| ~593–571 | Ezekiel |
| 586 | **Nebuchadnezzar conquers Jerusalem; second Babylonian exile** |
| ~540 | Second Isaiah |
| 538 | **Cyrus ushers Jews back to Judea; end of Babylonian exile** |
| ~520 | Haggai and Zechariah |
| ~500 | Obadiah |
| ~460 | Malachi |
| 400 | Joel |
| 300 | Book of **Jonah** written (~300–250 B.C.E.) |

The prophets of Israel, and especially the prophets whose writings appear in the *Tanakh,* wrote most of their prophecies in verse. Sometimes the prophets were very angry at the people and expressed this in their writings. At other times, they were very encouraging. Sometimes they spoke of doom and destruction, while at other times they were very hopeful and optimistic.

The prophets criticized kings, priests, and foreign gods. They told people how to behave. They warned people of what they were doing wrong. Because of these messages, most people didn't like the prophets. The prophets seem like a sad and lonely bunch of people.

Unlike the priests and (sometimes) the kings, prophecy was not passed on from parent to child. The *Tanakh* tells us that God called on them. And once called, they had little choice but to speak out for God.

To spread their message, the prophets used poetry as well as visions, metaphors, and personal stories. By "vision" we mean that the prophets sometimes described dreamlike experiences. An early example of a vision is Jacob's dream of a ladder going to heaven with angels coming down and going up. Isaiah, Ezekiel, and others from the Literary Prophets have similar stories of unusual meetings with God, angels, and other heavenly beings.

The message of the prophets covered many areas. To try to summarize everything that all the prophets wrote would be impossible. But the following are the main points that all the prophets taught:

- Stay true to God. Don't even pretend to be interested in other gods.

- Do what God wants. Be obedient to God, and follow God's will.

- Behave with justice, mercy, and right action.

- If you stray from the ways of God, you will be punished.

- The punishment may be exile from God and from your land.

- But after exile, if you return to God, God will return you to your kingdom, and it will be the way it was during the best of times when David was king.

*In this chapter, we reviewed the contents of the Torah and the Historical Prophets. In preparation for the Literary Prophets, we looked at the forms of Hebrew verse—couplets, beats, mood, image, and parallelism—as well as the messages of the prophets. In the next two chapters, we will begin looking at the writings of some of the Literary Prophets, beginning with Amos, Hosea, and Isaiah.*

# Chapter Thirteen

# AMOS AND HOSEA

*Up to this point, all the books we have looked at have told stories from the history of Israel. We have encountered many prophets, including Samuel, Nathan, Elijah, and Elisha. They were all characters or participants in the events described in the books. In this chapter we will look at two books written **by** prophets that, rather than telling histories, give us the speeches or sermons of the prophets.*

Amos and Hosea were two men who lived and wrote in Judah and Israel during the middle of the eighth century B.C.E., approximately a hundred years after the days of Elijah and Elisha, and two hundred years after King Solomon ruled.

Although their books are short—which is why they are included in the twelve "minor" prophets—their writing was very important. They had a new approach to God and religion, and they set the stage for "major" prophets like Isaiah and Jeremiah.

## Amos of Tekoa

If the books of the *Tanakh* had been sorted in the order that they were written, the Book of **Amos** would be the first of the Literary Prophets. Although he is not the first to appear in the *Tanakh,* Amos was the first of the prophets in the Bible whose speeches were written down and collected in a book.

Amos was a farmer from a desert settlement in the Southern Kingdom, but he moved to the Northern Kingdom. He wrote most of his prophecies about the Northern Kingdom. He didn't like what he saw there.

The people of Israel were overconfident. They thought that since they were God's chosen people, they were safe. They could do whatever they wanted. They were better than all the other nations. God would always be on their side, no matter what they did.

They were wrong.

Amos knew that Israel's God was really the God of all nations. If Israel behaved improperly, if they rejected God or mistreated the poor, God would punish them as God punished other nations. Amos wanted to warn the people of the Northern Kingdom to improve their behavior before it was too late.

In the opening of the Book of **Amos**, the prophet began by telling about all the bad things the other nations had done. He followed an interesting pattern, beginning:

*Thus said God:*

*For three sins of Damascus,*

*For four I will not take back punishment.*

AMOS 1:3

The "three—four" pattern is a figure of speech. It probably means that God was going to punish Damascus for its many sins. Even if it had only committed three or four transgressions, God would still follow through with the punishment.

The prophet went on:

*Thus said God:*

*For three sins of Gaza,*

*For four I will not take back punishment.*

AMOS 1:6

Amos then described the sin of the people of Gaza and their punishment. The Israelites probably enjoyed hearing this. Amos was telling them that God would punish all their enemies.

*Thus said God:*

*For three sins of Tyre,*

*For four I will not take back punishment.*

AMOS 1:9

*Thus said God:*

*For three sins of Edom,*

*For four I will not take back punishment.*

AMOS 1:11

*Thus said God:*

*For three sins of the Ammonites,*

*For four I will not take back punishment.*

AMOS 1:13

*Thus said God:*

*For three sins of Moab,*

*For four I will not take back punishment.*

AMOS 2:1

By this time, the people of the Northern Kingdom must have been cheering. Amos was telling them exactly what they wanted to hear. Their enemies would perish because God was on their side.

Then suddenly Amos surprised his audience by using the same pattern to describe their sister kingdom to the south:

*Thus said God:*
*For three sins of Judah,*
*For four I will not take back punishment:*
*Because they have rejected the Torah of*
    *God,*

*And have not observed God's laws;*
*They are confused by the false beliefs*
*That their ancestors kept.*
*I will send a fire on Judah*
*To burn the palaces of Jerusalem.*

                      AMOS 2:4–5

And finally, Amos turned his attention to the people of the Northern Kingdom themselves:

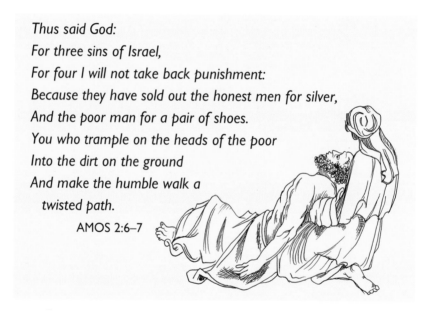

*Thus said God:*
*For three sins of Israel,*
*For four I will not take back punishment:*
*Because they have sold out the honest men for silver,*
*And the poor man for a pair of shoes.*
*You who trample on the heads of the poor*
*Into the dirt on the ground*
*And make the humble walk a*
    *twisted path.*
        AMOS 2:6–7

For several chapters, Amos described the punishment that Israel would suffer for their bad behavior. God would level their cities, destroy the palaces and altars, and take away all that the people had. Only a fraction of the people of Israel would survive that day of destruction, Amos warned.

But the message of Amos wasn't only doom and gloom. Israel had a choice. They could return to God, following God's laws of goodness, and life would continue for Israel. God did not want empty rituals. The sacrifices meant nothing to God without proper intention and good behavior:

*Seek good and not evil that you may live*
*And that God may truly be with you.*
*Hate evil and love good, and establish*
*    justice in the town square.*
*Then maybe God will be gracious to the*
*    survivors of Joseph.*

. . . . . . . . . . . . . . . . . . . . . . . . . . . . . . . . . . . .

*I hate, I reject your festivals,*
*I am not pleased by your ceremonies.*
*If you offer Me burnt offerings or meal*
*    offerings,*

*I will not accept them.*
*I pay no attention*
*To your gifts of livestock.*
*Spare Me the sound of your hymns*
*Don't make Me listen to the music of your*
*    harps.*
*But let justice well up like water,*
*Righteousness like a mighty stream.*

AMOS 5:14–15, 21–24

The above passage is full of beautiful examples of the poetry forms we discussed in the last chapter. Look for the parallelisms in the couplets. Underline the key words in each line that have a parallel in its partner line.

Find an image in the above passage. Copy the lines containing the image in the space below.

I hate, I reject your festivals

I am not pleased by your ceremonies

What does that image do? What do you think the effect is on the listener? What was the point made by Amos in writing down that image?

Makes you think that maybe someone gets angry and interrupts a holiday. The point was so that he was saying the person was angry at the person

# Hosea

Scholars and historians agree, of all the books of the Bible, **Hosea** is the most difficult to understand. We know almost nothing about the man who wrote this book, except that he wrote it about ten years or more after **Amos** was written. We aren't sure if the things he tells us about himself are real or if he made them up as part of his message.

There are things Hosea wrote that don't make sense to historians. He sometimes used metaphors and images that sound like they represent something, but no one knows what.

In the first three chapters of the Book of **Hosea**, the prophet tells us the sad story of his marriage. Now, it's important to recognize that even these details may have been made up in order for Hosea to express his point about God and Israel.

According to the story, God told Hosea to marry a woman who would not remain true to him. Hosea married the woman, named Gomer, realizing that she was the type of woman who would run off, flirt, and have affairs with other men. This made Hosea angry at times and sad at other times. There were occasions when Hosea wanted to kill his wife and others when he wanted to forgive her and have her come back to him.

When God first spoke to Hosea, God said, "Go out and marry a promiscuous woman. For the land will stray away from God." So he went and married Gomer daughter of Diblaim. She became pregnant and they had a son, and God told him, "Name the son Jezreel, for I will soon punish the House of Jehu for the bloody deeds at Jezreel, and I will put an end to the monarchy in the House of Israel. That day I will break the bow of Israel in the Jezreel Valley."

She once again became pregnant and had a daughter. God said, "Name her Lo-Ruhamah [Unaccepted], for I will no longer accept the House of Israel or pardon them. I will however accept the House of Judah, and I will give them victory with bow and sword and battle, by horses and riders.

Next she had another son, and God said, "Name him Lo-Ammi [Not My People], because you are not My people and I will not be your God."

HOSEA 1:2–9

After Hosea finishes telling us about this bad marriage, he explains to us that the marriage is the same as the relationship between God and Israel. God is the patient husband, and Israel is the unfaithful wife.

Before reading the words of Hosea, try to stretch your own imagination. How is God like a patient husband? How is Israel like an unfaithful wife?

| God—The Patient Husband | The People Israel—An Unfaithful Wife |
|---|---|
| | |

Whether the events in the previous passage actually happened, no one is sure. But Hosea certainly wrote it to give a message to the people of Israel. What was Hosea's purpose in comparing Israel to his wife, Gomer?

_____

_____

_____

# The Coming Fall of Israel

Hosea believed that the Northern Kingdom of Israel was soon to fall apart. Not only were they struggling under the control of Assyria, but they were weakening from within because—according to Hosea and other prophets—they had strayed from God.

Grapes were an important crop in Israel in both the north and the south. Grapes have a special importance to Jews, as the source of wine. The blessing over the fruit of the vine is called _Kiddush,_ from the Hebrew root for "holiness." It is no wonder that in the following text Hosea used the image of the grapevine to represent Israel.

As you read that text, be on the lookout for certain words and images. Several times Hosea mentions "altars" and "pillars." Tall stone pillars or obelisks were popular for the worship of illicit gods like Marduk and Asshur. The prophets hated any symbols that represented the worship of these Baalim.

Most of the prophets believed that sacrifice was overrated. They knew that God would rather have our good behavior—justice and kindness—than our burnt offerings. The prophets especially distrusted the altars set up in northern cities like Bethel.

Israel is a ravaged vine
And so is its fruit.
When he had plenty of fruit
He made many altars;
When his land was bountiful
Pillars abounded
But now that his branches are broken
He feels his guilt
He pulls down his own altars
Smashes his pillars.

...........................................

The people of Samaria fear
For the calf of Beth-Aven
Its people and its priests
Who were once its joy
Mourn for the glory
That has left it.
It shall be brought to Assyria
As gift to its king;

Ephraim shall be ashamed
And Israel will be upset
Because of his plans.
Samaria's king is vanishing
Like foam on water
The shrines of Beth-Aven shall be ruined,
The sin of Israel
Thorns and stickers
Will grow on their altars.
They shall ask the mountains, "Bury us!"
To the hills they will say, "Fall on us!"

HOSEA 10:1–2, 5–8

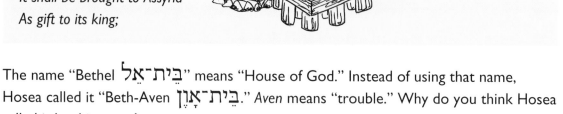

The name "Bethel בֵּית־אֵל" means "House of God." Instead of using that name, Hosea called it "Beth-Aven בֵּית־אָוֶן." *Aven* means "trouble." Why do you think Hosea called it by this name?

_____

_____

_____

Hosea was unhappy with the Israelites for many things. List some of them in the space below:

Three of the sins of Israel:

1. _____

2. _____

3. _____

Imagine that you are a press agent working for Hosea the prophet. Using his image of a ravaged vine, design a poster or billboard to help warn the people of Israel to change their ways before it is too late.

*Amos and Hosea were the earliest of the Literary Prophets whose writings we have in the Bible. Both men used poetry, visions, and stories to criticize the behavior of the Northern Kingdom of Israel and warn them to change their ways. In the next chapter, we will examine the writings of perhaps the greatest prophet of all—Isaiah.*

# Chapter Fourteen

## ISAIAH

*In all the previous chapters, we have read and learned about the many judges, kings, and prophets that led the people of Israel. In this chapter, we turn to the writings of the greatest prophet of the Bible. We will read what he wrote and learn about the times in which he lived. And we will ask the question of who Isaiah might have been and if he was really more than one person.*

The Book of **Isaiah** is the longest book of *N'vi-im* and one of the longest in the entire *Tanakh*. Like **Amos** and **Hosea**, this book is named for a prophet who wrote poetry and speeches. But the Book of **Isaiah** was written during a 150-year period and probably had several authors.

Here is what historians have suggested based on evidence found within the Bible texts and other historical evidence: There was a prophet named Isaiah ben Amoz. He lived in Judah, the Southern Kingdom, during the late eighth and early seventh centuries B.C.E., when the Northern Kingdom—Israel—was being conquered by Assyria. Isaiah ben Amoz delivered many sermons, speeches, and visions that were written down on scrolls by him and his followers.

Over 150 years later another prophet living in Babylon during the Babylonian exile wrote prophecies telling the people that God had not forgotten them and that they would be returned to their land. We don't know the name of this prophet. It is possible that he was also named Isaiah. This prophet was influenced by the ideas and the style of Isaiah ben Amoz. As a result, his teachings were combined with those of the earlier prophet. Historians call him "Second Isaiah" or "Deutero-Isaiah."

Finally, there was a third prophet who lived in Judah after the Babylonian exile. He shared many of the themes, language, and concerns of the other two. Many of his writings were also included in the Book of **Isaiah**. As the name of this prophet is also not known, we refer to him and his writings as "Third Isaiah" or "Trito-Isaiah."

The entire book is not neatly divided, so it is hard to tell exactly where one writer stopped and the next one began. Nevertheless, the Book of **Isaiah** as we have it today holds together as a collection of ideas about God and the future of the Israelite people. As we read and study **Isaiah**, we can imagine, as our ancestors have for more than 2,500 years, that its sixty-six chapters were written by one author who was guided by the spirit of God.

# What Did Isaiah Have to Say?

Isaiah wrote some of the strongest words ever written about God, religion, and justice. His prophecies included pleas to the people to behave properly and act kindly. He wasn't shy about telling the people of Judah what God expected of them. He told of his visions of God, and images of an apocalypse or end of days that might occur because of the failure of Israel to keep God's laws, and of the return of a great kingdom under a king descended from David.

Isaiah also had a message about monotheism that changed the way we think about God. Isaiah's message begins:

> These are the prophecies of Isaiah son of Amoz, who prophesied about Judah and Jerusalem during the reigns of Kings Uzziah [or Azariah], Jotham, Ahaz, and Hezekiah of Judah:
>
> Listen, heaven. Pay attention, earth.
> God has spoken:
> "I took care of children. I brought them up,
> But they have rebelled against Me!
> While an ox knows its owner,
> And a donkey knows its master's barn,
> Israel doesn't know.
> My people do not think!"
>
> ISAIAH 1:1–3

Isaiah then told the people that God did not want empty and meaningless sacrifices. What God truly wanted from us is to "stop doing evil, learn to do good, devote yourself to justice, help those who have been hurt, guard the rights of the orphan, and defend the cause of the widow" (Isaiah 1:16–17).

When Isaiah called the people with the names Sodom and Gomorrah in the following passage, he was comparing them to two cities from the time of Abraham. These cities were so evil, the Torah tells us, that God completely destroyed them. Just as "Jezebel" has become a symbol for a cruel woman, "Sodom and Gomorrah" are symbols of totally evil and corrupt societies.

> Listen to the word of God, leaders of
>     Sodom!
> Pay attention to God's teaching, people of
>     Gomorrah!
> What need do I have for your sacrifices?
>     says God.
> I have had My fill of burnt offerings of
>     rams,
>
> The fat of your cattle, the blood of bulls.
> I have no delight in lambs or goats.
> Who asked you to come before Me?
> Don't trample through My halls any more.
> Bringing offerings is empty,
> Incense bothers Me.
> New Moon and Shabbat
> Are false ceremonies

That I cannot allow!
Your New Moons and celebrations
Fill Me with disgust.
They bother me,
I cannot stand them.
And when you lift up your hands,
I will look the other way.
You pray a lot, but I will not listen.
Your hands are dirty with crime,

Wash yourself clean.
Do no more evil deeds
Ever in My sight.
Stop doing evil,
Learn to do good.
Devote yourself to justice.
Help those who have been hurt.
Guard the rights of the orphan,
Defend the cause of the widow.

ISAIAH 1:10–17

# Isaiah's Call for Justice

The message of Isaiah could also be upbeat and positive. The prophet was inviting people to follow the path of God and goodness. He promised that if we did, our world would be a wonderful place for everyone.

The following passage begins with a call to the people of Israel and Judah to join him. The peace will begin in Jerusalem. The "Mount of God" refers to the hill where the Temple stood. The "House of the God of Jacob" is the Temple itself. But the peace would spread throughout the world, to "many nations" and "many peoples."

Come, let us go to the Mount of God
To the House of the God of Jacob
That God may teach us the way,
And that we may walk in God's paths.
For teaching shall come out of Zion
And the word of God from Jerusalem.
So God will judge over many nations

And counsel the many peoples.
They shall beat their swords into
    plowshares
And their spears into pruning hooks.
Nation shall not lift up sword against
    nation
They shall never again know war.

ISAIAH 2:3–4

The above passage is full of beautiful images. Some of those words have become a part of our regular worship service. Read over the passage again. Choose two to four lines, and design a billboard or a T-shirt design on the next page using those lines.

## Isaiah's Revelation

In addition to Isaiah's practical political teachings about peace and justice, the prophet also wrote about what it means to be holy. This next passage seems like a strange dream in which Isaiah sees God on a throne. He describes seeing some creatures called "seraphim." These appear to be angelic creatures, similar to the cherubim, but with six wings, and bodies possibly made of fire.

In the year that King Uzziah died, I saw my God seated on a high and lofty throne. God's robe filled the Temple. Seraphim stood by, each with six wings. The first pair of wings covered their faces, the second pair covered their legs, and with the third pair they could fly.

They said to each other:

"Holy Holy Holy is God of all being,

The whole earth is filled with Your glory!"
The pillars shook at the sound, and the Temple was filling with smoke.

I cried: "Woe is me, I am doomed!
My lips are not clean, I live among people
   of unclean lips.
But with my own eyes I have seen the God
   of all being."

Then one of the seraphim flew over to

me with a burning coal, taken from the altar with a pair of tongs. He touched it to my lips and said:

*"Now that this has touched your lips,*
*Your guilt shall be gone*
*And your sin washed away."*

Then I heard the voice of God saying, "Whom shall I send? Who will go for us?"

*And I said, "Here I am. Send me."*
*And God said, "Go, and tell the people that*
*they surely hear, but don't understand.*
*They certainly see, but they don't get it.*
*Make their minds dull.*

*Close their ears and seal their eyes.*
*If they see with their eyes*
*And hear with their ears,*
*They will understand with their minds*
*And repent and save themselves."*

*I asked, "How long, God?"*

*God replied, "Until the towns are ruined*
*and empty.*
*The houses have no people,*
*The land is wasted and desolate.*
*God will banish the population*
*And there will be many vacant sites in the*
*land."*

ISAIAH 6:1–12

This vision has puzzled and enchanted readers for thousands of years. The verses in which the seraphim said "Holy Holy Holy" has become a part of Jewish daily worship. They are part of the *K'dushah* prayer within the *Amidah (T'filah)* section of the service.

KADOSH   KADOSH   KADOSH
קָדוֹשׁ   קָדוֹשׁ   קָדוֹשׁ
ADONAI TZ'VAOT
M'LO CHOL HAARETZ K'VODO

After hearing those words, Isaiah reacted by crying:

*"Woe is me, I am doomed!*
*My lips are not clean, I live among people*
*of unclean lips.*

*But with my own eyes I have seen the God*
*of all being."*

ISAIAH 6:5

What do you think Isaiah meant by this? What did he mean about the unclean lips? Why would he consider himself doomed after seeing God with his own eyes?

# Isaiah and the K'dushah

We sanctify Your name on earth, even as all things, to the ends of time and space, proclaim Your holiness, and in the words of the prophet we say:

*Holy Holy Holy is the God of all being!*

*The whole earth is filled with Your glory!*

Source of our strength, Sovereign God, how majestic is Your name in all the earth!

Praised be the glory of God in heaven and earth.

Jewish law teaches that any number of people can pray the daily services. But five parts of the service may only be said when a minyan of ten is present. These are the *Kaddish*, the *Bar'chu*, the repetition of the *Amidah*, the Torah reading, and the K'dushah.

The *K'dushah* is the third blessing in the *Amidah*, an important section of every prayer service. Many people consider the *K'dushah* to be the very heart of the *Amidah*, with its flowing poetry, its memorable melody, and its message of holiness. At the center of the *Amidah* is a repetition of the words from Isaiah 6:3.

As you read the above passage, taken from the Shabbat Morning Service in *Gates of Prayer*, locate and mark a circle around the verses taken from Isaiah.

## Praying on Tiptoes

Here's a custom you might have seen: it is traditional to rise up on tiptoes three times, once each time the word *Kadosh* is said during the *K'dushah*. This is to imitate the flying and fluttering seraphim in Isaiah's vision.

# Apocalypse

The Book of **Isaiah** contains elaborate descriptions of what the world may be like if God is compelled to punish the world. As in the story of Noah, God will cleanse the earth by destroying all that is evil. And when the cleaning is complete, the world will be able to begin fresh and new.

Stories like this of the destruction and renewal of the earth are called "apocalyptic," from the Greek word meaning "to uncover." This event of the end of days is called an "apocalypse." Chapters 24 through 27 of Isaiah describe such an event. It begins with the violent cleansing:

*God will strip the earth bare,*
*And lay it waste,*
*And twist the surface,*
*And scatter its inhabitants.*
*Laymen and priests will suffer the same,*
*Slave and master,*
*Maid and mistress,*
*Buyer and seller,*
*Lender and borrower,*
*Banker and debtor.*
*The earth shall be totally bare.*

*It shall be completely plundered,*
*For it is God who has said this.*
*The earth is withered,*
*The world is fading.*
*Sky and earth fade.*
*The earth was contaminated*
*By its inhabitants.*
*They ignored Torah,*
*Violated laws,*
*Broke the ancient covenant.*

ISAIAH 24:1–5

When all seems destroyed and lost, a new, beautiful era will begin, like grapevines sprouting in spring:

*In that day,*
*The earth shall sing*
*Vineyard of Delight*
*I, Adonai, guard over it.*
*I water it every moment*
*No harm shall come to it.*
*I watch it night and day.*
*There is no anger in Me.*
*If someone offers Me thorns and thistles,*

*I will march to battle against him*
*And set them all on fire.*
*But whoever holds tightly to Me*
*Will be My friend*
*Will be My friend.*
*In the days to come, Jacob will lay roots,*
*Israel shall sprout and blossom,*
*And the face of the earth*
*Will be covered with fruit.*

ISAIAH 27:2–6

After the verse "But whoever holds tightly to Me," Isaiah repeats the next line twice:

Will be My friend
Will be My friend

*Yaaseh shalom li*
*Yaaseh shalom li*

This line could also be translated as "he will make peace with Me."

What do you think it means?

_____

_____

Why was the line repeated?

_____

_____

# Monotheism: One God Alone!

The term "monotheism" means belief in one god. This belief is very important in Judaism. But the belief was never so clear until Isaiah began prophesying. Until that time, Israelites believed that their God, whose proper name was Yahweh יְהֹוָה, but was also known as *Adonai* יְיָ and *Elohim* אֱלֹהִים, was the Number One God, the Top God, the best and most powerful of the gods. From the time of Moses, they understood that their God was invisible and shouldn't be carved as a statue. But they didn't say that there were no other gods in existence.

Isaiah changed that. His teaching, that God was the only God, shapes the way we understand monotheism today.

Listen, now, My servant Jacob,
Israel whom I have chosen!
God, your Maker speaks,
Your Creator who cared for you since birth.
Do not be afraid, My servant Jacob,
Jeshurun [Israel] whom I have chosen,
Just as I pour water on thirsty soil,
Rain on dry land,
I will pour My spirit on your children,
My blessing on your descendants.
They will sprout like grass,
Like willows on a brook.

I am the first and I am the last,
There is no god but me.

The idol-makers
They all work for nothing.
The thing they worship
Can do no good.
As they themselves know.
They don't look or think,
So they shall be shamed.
Why would anyone design a god
Or carve a stone,
That can do no good?

ISAIAH 44:1–4, 6, 9–10

In the above text, the author uses an image of water or rain. What does the water symbolize? Why is the author using this imagery?

_____

_____

What do you think God meant in saying, "I am the first and I am the last"?

_____

_____

Isaiah has strong words about idols. What is his message to people who make and worship handmade gods?

_____

_____

_Although the Book of **Isaiah** was probably written by several people over a century and a half, it still remains one of the most central, most beautiful, and most original writings about God in the Bible or anywhere. The prophet(s) Isaiah still challenges us to act justly, to be holy, and to look forward to a positive future with God. In the next chapter, we will learn about the events that took place after the time of Isaiah that shook the people of Israel, nearly destroying them before allowing them to sprout again like a fresh vineyard._

# Chapter Fifteen

# THE END OF AN ERA

*For thousands of years, Jews have looked back at the kingdom of David as the best years—the Golden Age—of Jewish history. In some ways, the monarchy of David and Solomon deserves to be remembered this way. In other ways, it has been exaggerated and romanticized by time. Even after civil war divided the nation into Judah and Israel, the period of the monarchy was the last time until 1948 that Jews had a land and a country they could call their own. Just as Adam and Eve were cast out of the Garden of Eden, first the Kingdom of Israel and then the Kingdom of Judah were thrown into exile. In this chapter, we will look at the events that shaped the rest of the Bible and gave shape to the Jewish religion as we know it today.*

It was an age of empires.

One strong nation with a strong ruler would begin conquering smaller nations until it had control of the entire known world—or until a stronger nation would conquer it. It was an ancient game of military monopoly.

When a nation joined the empire, it was required to pay tribute—goods, money, and soldiers—to the capital of the empire. In a similar manner, modern governments require their citizens to pay taxes. What do you think your government uses tax money to buy? See if you can list three items, services, or buildings that are paid for with tax dollars.

1. _____

2. _____

3. _____

Egypt was conquering smaller kingdoms to the south. Assyria was trying to take over Syria in the north and Philistia to the west. Israel and Judah were caught in the middle.

What do you think it was like being two small countries stuck between two warring empires?

_____

_____

In the years after the death of King Ahab, there were many skirmishes between Israel, Judah, and their neighboring kingdoms. Moabite invaders would come in year after year. Israel and Judah were both becoming weaker and weaker. King Hazael of Aram (Syria) kept attacking both Israelite kingdoms. Syria, which had its capital in Damascus, was a close neighbor to Israel and Judah.

Imagine that Israel and Judah are a brother and sister who often fight with each other. Syria was their next-door neighbor who was sometimes friendly with one, sometimes friendly with the other, but seldom friendly with both at the same time.

Can you think of a similar situation in your own life? Consider a relationship in school, your neighborhood, or home where friendships shift. Describe it below:

_____

_____

# The Coming of the Assyrians

A new empire was rising. The Assyrians were actually a very old nation. Assyria (not the same as Syria, even though the names are similar) had been a great nation for more than a thousand years by the time Ahaz became king in Judah. Their territory was about 500 miles to the east of the Jordan River, in what is now Iraq. But now, with a new king, the Assyrians were getting themselves ready to be the next world empire. The Book of **Second Kings** describes it:

In the twenty-seventh year of King Jeroboam of Israel, Azariah [or Uzziah] son of King Amaziah of Judah became king. He was sixteen years old when he became king, and he ruled for fifty-two years in Jerusalem. His mother was Jecoliah of Jerusalem.

He did what was pleasing to God, just as his father Amaziah had done. But he did not remove the foreign shrines. The people continued to make sacrifices and offerings at these shrines.

God struck the king with leprosy, which he suffered until his death. He lived in seclusion while his son, Jotham, was in charge of the palace and governed the people of the land....

In the fifty-second year of King Azariah of Judah, Pekah son of Remaliah became king over Israel and Samaria. He ruled for twenty years and did what was displeasing to God. During the reign of King Pekah of Israel, King Tiglath-Pileser of Assyria captured the entire territory of Naphtali around the Galilee and sent them away to Assyria.

II KINGS 15:1–5, 27–29

The new king of Assyria—Shalmaneser V—decided that he wanted all the kingdoms in the Middle East under his control. He wanted these other countries to send him money and gifts, and he wanted their armies to help him conquer more countries.

Under the rule of the Assyrian kings Tiglath-Pileser, Shalmaneser V, and Sargon II, the Assyrian empire spread over a large territory. Using the five phases in the box on the right on page 141, color in Assyria's progress.

| The Growth of the Assyrian Empire | | |
| --- | --- | --- |
| Phase 1: | Urartu | Blue |
| Phase 2: | Northern Syria Damascus Gaza | Green |
| Phase 3: | Babylon | Red |
| Phase 4: | Syria Israel | Purple |
| Phase 5: | Cyprus Armenia Babylonia | Yellow |

In the next text, we will see how King Shalmaneser of Assyria took control of the Northern Kingdom and made King Hoshea of Israel his servant. Then, after nine years, a new king arose in Assyria who was even fiercer than Shalmaneser. His name was Sargon, and he obliterated the Northern Kingdom.

In the twelfth year of King Ahaz of Judah, Hoshea son of Elah became king over Israel in Samaria. He ruled for nine years. He did what was displeasing to God, though not as bad as the kings of Israel who came before him. King Shalmaneser marched against him, and Hoshea became his servant and paid him tribute.

But the king of Assyria found out that Hoshea had been dealing behind his back. He found out that Hoshea had paid tribute to King So of Egypt rather than paying tribute to the king of Assyria as he had in previous years. The king of Assyria arrested him and put him in prison. Then the king of Assyria led a march against the entire land. He came to Samaria and attacked it for three years. During the ninth year of King Hoshea, the king of Assyria captured Samaria. He sent all the Israelites to Assyria and settled them in Halah, at the Habor, and the Gozan River, and in the towns of Media.

All of this happened because the Israelites had sinned against God, who had freed them from the land of Egypt, from the hand of Pharaoh. They had worshiped other gods and followed the customs of the nations who had lived there before. The Israelites did things to God that were not right. They set up shrines in all their settlements and cities; they set up pillars and sacred posts for themselves on every high hill and under every leafy tree. They offered sacrifices at all the shrines, like the other nations. They worshiped idols, which God had told them not to do.

God had warned Israel and Judah by every prophet and every seer, saying, "Turn back from your wicked ways and observe My mitzvot and My laws, as it is in the Torah that I commanded your ancestors."

But the people did not obey. They had stiff necks like their ancestors and didn't have faith in God. They ignored God's laws and the covenant made with their ancestors. They rejected all the mitzvot of God. They made metal idols for themselves—two calves. They made a sacred post and bowed down to all sorts of gods and worshiped Baal. They put their sons and daughters to the fire and practiced magic and fortune-telling. They did what was displeasing to God, making God angry.

God was furious at Israel. God banished Israel until no one was left but the tribe of Judah.

II KINGS 17:1–18

Why was God angry at the nation of Israel? What, according to the text, did they do wrong?

_____

_____

What did God do to punish the nation of Israel?

_____

_____

# "Ten Lost Tribes" of Israel

The reign of King Sargon of Assyria completely and permanently destroyed the Kingdom of Israel. Sargon forced many of those northern Israelites who had survived the defeat to leave their land and be relocated in a far-off region of the Assyrian empire. His goal was to split them up and separate them from their land and their customs so that Assyria would have no need to worry about future rebellions.

For the most part, Sargon's strategy worked. Within a generation, anyone who had come from the Northern Kingdom of Israel had become a part of another nation.

Some northerners joined the Kingdom of Judah, while others were absorbed into other nations and regions where all memory of them gradually vanished, giving rise to legends about the "ten lost tribes."

Still other northerners remained in the region, deprived of statehood. They were called "Samaritans," named for their former capital, Samaria. A small community of Samaritans still exists today in the State of Israel.

The Rabbis of the Talmud had many theories as to where the lost tribes had gone. Some said that they went to Africa. Others said that they crossed the mythical river of Sambatyon, which rushes with such a current that no one can cross it except on Shabbat, when Torah forbids it. Perhaps they wound up in Turkey. Or as Rabbi Sh'muel bar Nachman said, "a cloud came down and concealed them."

What do you think happened to the ten lost tribes? See if you can devise a theory of your own.

_____

_____

All that remained of the descendants of Jacob were the people of the tribes of Judah and Benjamin, and apparently Levites and the members of Simeon that had been absorbed into Judah.

# Life Goes on in Judah

After the year 722 B.C.E., all that was left of the Israelite people were the Kingdom of Judah and the scattered Israelites who lived with them. Because of this, all Israelites came to be called *Y'hudim* יְהוּדִים—Judahites. This name—*Y'hudim*—evolved into the word "Jew." Therefore, from this point, it is fair to use the terms "Jews" and "Israelites" interchangeably.

By 620 B.C.E. the Assyrian empire was crumbling. In 610 B.C.E., Egypt destroyed Assyria and took over their former territories, becoming imperial head of most of the Middle East, including Judah.

Then, in 605 B.C.E., a new empire arose. The empire, led by Nebuchadnezzar, came to be called the New Babylonian Empire and began taking control of the kingdoms that had been first under the Assyrians and then the Egyptians.

# Babylonian Exile

King Nebuchadnezzar of Babylon ruled over all that had been Assyria. He held control over three kings of Judah: Jehoiakim, Jehoiachin, and Zedekiah. When King Zedekiah tried to free Judah from Babylon, the Kingdom of Judah came to an end.

Zedekiah rebelled against the king of Babylon, and in the ninth year of his reign, on the tenth day of the tenth month, Nebuchadnezzar attacked Jerusalem with his entire army. He besieged it and built fortification all around the city, starving the people inside.

Finally the city walls were breached. The Chaldean soldiers captured the king and brought him to the king of Babylon at Riblah, and they put him on trial. They killed Zedekiah's sons before his eyes and then put out Zedekiah's eyes. They chained him up and brought him to Babylon.

On the seventh day of the fifth month—during the nineteenth year of King Nebuchadnezzar of Babylon—the Babylonian officer Nebuzaradan came to Jerusalem. He burned the House of God, the king's palace, and all the houses in Jerusalem. All the Chaldean forces that were with him helped tear down the walls of Jerusalem on every side. Nebuzaradan, the chief of guards, took all those people who were left in the city into exile. Only the poorest people were left to take care of the land.

II KINGS 25:1–12

# Lamentations

The Book of **Lamentations**—or *Eichah*—is a collection of five very sad and beautiful poems about the destruction of Jerusalem. **Lamentations,** which is found in the *K'tuvim* section of the Bible, is one of the five *m'gillot*. We read this *m'gillah* on Tishah B'Av, the Ninth of Av, a solemn day on which we remember the Babylonian exile and other tragedies of the Jewish people.

We will learn more about **Lamentations** and the other *m'gillot* later in this textbook.

Imagine that you and your family were forced to leave your home and your community. What sort of poem would you write to express your sadness? Use the space below to write some verses of your own.

_____

_____

_____

_____

_____

The following passage from **Lamentations** gives us an idea of the sadness of the people after being expelled from their homeland:

God in anger
Has shamed fair Zion,
Has thrown the majesty of Israel
From heaven to earth.
God did not remember the Temple
On the day of wrath.

God laid waste without pity
All the homes of Jacob.
God toppled in anger
Fair Judah's strongholds.
God brought down in shame
The kingdom and its leaders.

LAMENTATIONS 2:1–2

And in the Book of **Psalms** we find these verses:

| | |
|---|---|
| *By the rivers of Babylon,* | *If I forget you, O Jerusalem,* |
| *There we sat,* | *May my right hand wither,* |
| *We sat and wept,* | *May my tongue stick in my mouth* |
| *As we thought of Zion.* | *If I stop thinking of you,* |
| PSALM 137:1 | *If I do not keep Jerusalem in mind* |
| | *Even at my happiest hour.* |
| | PSALM 137:5 |

## The Legacy of Exile

As sad and tragic as the Babylonian exile was, if it had not happened, most of us would not recognize Judaism today. It was during and after the exile that most of our prophetic books and the *K'tuvim* were written down or composed. Scholars believe that the final parts of the Torah were also composed at this time and that many of the ancient parts of the Torah were given their final form at this time.

With the Temple destroyed, Jews were unable to make offerings. Prayer and the study of Torah became the main religious activities. During this time, new Jewish gathering houses began popping up, buildings that eventually came to be called by the Greek name "synagogue."

**How was Jewish life different after the exile? What changes occurred during that time?**

_____

_____

The Babylonian exile was without a doubt the most important event in shaping Judaism. The Israelite religion had previously been confined to the land of Israel, but because of the Babylonian exile, Judaism spread throughout the entire known world.

*In this chapter, we learned about the end of two Israelite kingdoms: the destruction of the Northern Kingdom of Israel by the Assyrians in 722 B.C.E., and the capture of Jerusalem and the Babylonian exile in 586 B.C.E. These two tragic events gave shape to the Jewish religion as we know it today. In the next several chapters, we will read about how these events affected the prophets who lived through them.*

# Chapter Sixteen

## JEREMIAH

*Two chapters back, we read the words of Isaiah, who warned the Israelites, north and south, to return faithfully to God or their nation would be destroyed. In the previous chapter, we learned about the destruction of the Northern Kingdom by Assyria, and we read of how 150 years later, the Southern Kingdom, Judah, was forced into exile and the Temple destroyed by the Babylonians. In the years before the Babylonian exile, a prophet named Jeremiah spread the word to the people of Judah, whether they wanted to hear it or not.*

The prophets were unusual people. But Jeremiah was particularly different. He was quiet, humble, and very sad. It seems he had few friends, and he made many enemies because of the things he said.

Most of the Literary Prophets were from the Southern Kingdom of Judah. Jeremiah was from the tribe of Benjamin and had ties to the former Northern Kingdom.

Jeremiah lived through an interesting and sometimes difficult time, as we'll see from his writings. The Kingdom of Judah was in a crisis similar to what the Northern Kingdom had suffered 150 years earlier. Jeremiah's writings were written in the years just before and during the Babylonian exile that we read about in the last chapter.

Jeremiah's opinions went against those of nearly everyone around him. His speeches often got him in trouble. He was frequently on the run and hiding from authorities, and he did spend some time in jail.

Other prophets, including Jeremiah, had made enemies with kings and priests. But Jeremiah made enemies even with other prophets.

## The Call of Jeremiah

In modern English, another word for "job" or "occupation" is the term "vocation." Schools that train people for specific jobs are called "vocational schools." The word "vocation"—from the same root as "vocal" and "voice"—means "calling." It was once believed (and, who knows, it may be true) that every person is called on by God to fulfill a specific profession—whether he or she is a doctor, a teacher, a scientist, or a farmer.

Have you ever felt "called" for a certain task? Even if you are young, there is probably some hobby, some profession, or some interest that pulls at you. What do you think your "calling" might be?

_____

_____

The term "calling" still has its original meaning when we talk about the prophets. In the case of each prophet, God called on him or her, instructing that they were meant for a career of being God's spokesperson.

Jeremiah's calling may not be as dramatic as Isaiah's vision of God on a throne surrounded by chanting seraphim. But it does give us a good understanding—without all the fireworks—of what it might have been like to be called on as a spokesperson for God.

During the 1950s and 1960s, Sheldon H. Blank, a rabbi and a professor of Bible, wrote several books about the prophets. According to Professor Blank, there are four features that are found in nearly every story of a prophet's calling.

These are the four features of the stories about a prophet's vocation:

1. God commands the prophet to go.

2. The prophet doesn't want to go or feels that he or she is not good enough to go. For example, Moses told God three times that he wouldn't be a good prophet. Isaiah said that he was a man of unclean lips.

3. The prophet learns that his or her job is to speak for God. God will put something in the prophet's mouth or tell the prophet to say only what God tells him or her to say.

4. The job of a prophet is very difficult. Being a prophet meant that life would be hard and that people would hate you.

To get a better understanding of the elements of a prophet's call, match the four features on the following page with the text from the story of Moses that illustrates it.

| | |
|---|---|
| God commands the prophet to go. | Moses said to God, "I have never been a man of words, either in the past or now. I am slow of speech and slow of tongue." <div align="right">EXODUS 4:10</div> |
| The prophet doesn't want to go. | In the desert, the whole Israelite community grumbled against Moses and Aaron, saying, "We should have stayed to die in Egypt rather than coming out here to starve in the desert!" <div align="right">EXODUS 16:2–3</div> |
| The prophet learns that his or her job is to speak for God. | God told Moses, "Go to Pharaoh and say to him, 'This is what the God of the Hebrews says: Let My people go!'" <div align="right">EXODUS 9:1</div> |
| The job of a prophet is very difficult. | [God said to Moses:] "Come. I will send you to Pharaoh, and you shall free My people." <div align="right">EXODUS 3:10</div> |

All these features can be seen clearly in the story of the calling of Jeremiah. As you read this text, watch for the four features of the prophetic call:

These are the words of Jeremiah son of Hilkiah, one of the priests of Anathoth in the territory of Benjamin. The word of God came to him during the time of King Josiah of Judah, King Jehoiakim of Judah, and King Zedekiah of Judah.

The word of God came to me:

"I chose you before I had created you in the womb. Before you were born, I chose you. I appointed you a prophet of the nations."

I said, "*Adonai*, God, I don't know how to speak, for I am still immature."

God said to me, "Don't say that you are immature. You will go where I send you and say what I command. Do not be afraid, for I will protect you."

God put out a hand and touched my mouth. Then God said to me, "With this I put My words in your mouth. See, I appoint you today over nations and kingdoms.

*"To uproot and pull down,*
*To destroy and overthrow,*
*To build and to plant."*

JEREMIAH 1:1–10

In the spaces below, copy the verse or sentence from the text that best illustrates the four features of the prophetic call.

1. God commands the prophet to go where he is sent.

_____

_____

_____

_____

2. The prophet is unwilling or feels not good enough.

_____

_____

_____

_____

3. God gives the prophet the words to say.

_____

_____

_____

_____

4. The job will be difficult.

_____

_____

_____

_____

Jeremiah's revelation ends with the following lines:

*To uproot and pull down,*
*To destroy and overthrow,*
*To build and to plant.*

What could these words be referring to? What was God asking Jeremiah to uproot, destroy, and then rebuild?

_____

_____

_____

# The Temple Sermon

One of the most important speeches of Jeremiah was this one, delivered outside the Temple of Jerusalem. Prophets in the past had criticized the Temple and the empty and hypocritical behavior that went on inside. Jeremiah took his complaints directly to the Temple, and he ultimately wound up a fugitive.

This is what *Adonai Tz'vaot*, the God of Israel, says:

"Mend your ways and your actions and I will let you live in this land. Don't put your faith in lies, telling yourself, 'God's Temple! God's Temple! This is God's Temple!'

"If you really mend your ways and your actions:

"If you are just and fair with each other,
If you do not oppress the stranger, the orphan, and the widow,
If you kill no innocent person,
If you do not follow other gods,
Only then will I let you live here, in the land that I gave to your fathers for all time.

See, you are relying on lies that will not do you any good.
Would you steal,
Murder,
Commit adultery,
Lie under oath,
Sacrifice to Baal,
Follow other unproven gods—
And then come to My Temple and stand before Me, and say that you are safe here?
Safe for what? Wickedness?
Do you think the House that bears My name should be a den of thieves?
I have been watching!"

JEREMIAH 7:3–11

According to Jeremiah, what were the people of Judah doing that was wrong?

_____

_____

What should the people of Judah have been doing that would have "pleased" God?

_____

_____

Why did Jeremiah call the Temple a "den of thieves"?

_____

_____

# The Coming of Nebuchadnezzar

The king of Babylon who invaded Judah is usually called Nebuchadnezzar in the Bible. In his own language he was called Nabu-kudurri-usur. He was the leader of the Chaldean nation, and with his power he was able to establish the New Babylonian Empire, which took over Assyria and all the smaller nations that had been in its control.

In **Jeremiah,** his name is spelled Nebuchad**r**ezzar, with an "r," making it closer to the Babylonian name than Nebuchad**n**ezzar with an "n."

Jeremiah gave a stern warning that the Babylonians, led by Nebuchadnezzar, would conquer the Kingdom of Judah:

Here is what came to Jeremiah from God when King Nebuchadrezzar of Babylon was waging war against Jerusalem:

"Go to King Zedekiah of Judah, tell him: 'This is what God says: I am going to hand this city over to the king of Babylon. He will burn it down. You will not escape, but will be captured and handed over to him. You will meet the king of Babylon face-to-face, and you will speak with him. But hear this, King Zedekiah of Judah: You will not die by the sword. You will die a peaceful death. Incense will be burned in your honor as was done for your ancestors. I make this promise,' said God."

JEREMIAH 34:1–5

# A Prophet on the Run

Jeremiah had made so many enemies during his career as a prophet that it was getting hard for him to get his message out. No one would listen to him. He was not allowed to enter the Temple or to speak in public.

Why was Jeremiah not allowed to speak? Who wouldn't want to hear Jeremiah's prophecies? Why not?

_____

_____

Jeremiah hired a scribe, Baruch son of Neriah, to serve as his assistant, his secretary, and his messenger.

In the fourth year of King Jehoiakim son of Josiah of Judah, the word of God came to Jeremiah:

"Get a scroll and write on it all the words that I have spoken to you, regarding Israel, Judah, and all the other nations. When the House of Judah hear of all the disasters I plan to bring upon them, they will turn back from their wicked way, and I will pardon their sins."

Jeremiah called Baruch son of Neriah, and Baruch wrote down on the scroll everything Jeremiah dictated to him, all the words that God said.

Jeremiah told Baruch, "I am in hiding. I cannot go to the Temple. Would you go and read aloud the words of God that you wrote on the scroll? Read it to everyone in the Temple during a fast day. That way, all the people from the neighboring towns will be there."

Baruch son of Neriah did as Jeremiah the prophet had told him, and he read the words of God from the scroll at the Temple. There was a fast to God in Jerusalem during the ninth month of the fifth year of King Jehoiakim's reign. It was then that Baruch went to a chamber in the upper court, near the new entrance of the Temple, and read the words of Jeremiah to all the people in the Temple....

[After the king heard about the scroll] the king ordered that the scroll be brought to him. This was during the ninth month, and the king was staying at his winter house at the time.

Jehudi [one of the king's officers] read the scroll to the king. Every couple of columns, the king would cut that piece of the scroll with a knife and throw it into the fire in his oven. Soon the entire scroll had been burned in the oven. The king and those around him showed no fear. Three of his officials begged him not to burn the scroll, but he would not listen to them.

The king ordered that his men arrest Baruch the scribe and Jeremiah the prophet. But God hid them....

Jeremiah got another scroll and gave it to Baruch the scribe. At Jeremiah's dictation, he wrote the entire text of the scroll that King Jehoiakim had burned, with similar material added.

JEREMIAH 36:1–10, 21–26, 32

What was written on the scroll?

_____

_____

Why did King Jehoiakim burn the scroll?

_____

_____

# Jeremiah's Arrest

In the year 597 B.C.E., the Babylonian empire took control of Judah. King Jehoiachin, the son of Jehoiakim, was removed from the throne by Babylonian officials and was replaced by King Zedekiah. Jehoiachin and all the Judean leaders were taken to Babylon as prisoners. (Ten years later, in the Babylonian exile, the same thing would happen, on a much larger and more devastating scale.)

King Zedekiah was no different than the kings who came before him. He ignored Jeremiah's warnings.

During a raid by the Babylonians (called "Chaldeans" in this text), Jeremiah tried to leave Jerusalem and was caught by one of the king's officers.

Jeremiah was leaving Jerusalem to stay with someone in the territory of Benjamin. When he got to the Benjamin Gate, a guard officer named Irijah arrested him, saying, "You are under arrest for defecting to the Chaldeans!"

Jeremiah answered, "That's not true. I am not defecting to the Chaldeans."

But Irijah ignored him. He arrested Jeremiah and brought him to the authorities.

The authorities were very angry with Jeremiah. They beat him and put him in prison. Jeremiah remained there in solitary confinement for a long time.

Eventually, King Zedekiah had Jeremiah brought to him secretly so that he could question him. "Is there any word from God?" he asked.

"You will be captured by the king of Babylon," he said. "Now, what have I done to you and your people that you have put me in jail? Where are all the prophets who said that the king of Babylon would never attack you here? Please listen to me, your majesty. Don't send me back to that prison to die."

So King Zedekiah had Jeremiah moved to a nicer prison compound and arranged that fresh bread be brought to him every day until there was no bread left in the city. Jeremiah stayed in prison.

JEREMIAH 37:12–21

Why was Jeremiah arrested?

_____

_____

What was Jeremiah's message to King Zedekiah?

_____

_____

Jeremiah was the saddest of the prophets. In fact, other than Job (whom we will meet in a later chapter), Jeremiah is probably the most unhappy man in the entire *Tanakh*.

Jeremiah spent years on the run and was tortured in jail; people hated him wherever he went. And all this for saying what God had told him to say. Sadly, his warnings all came true. Jerusalem was destroyed, and Judah taken captive for nearly fifty years.

But in all his depression, there was a glimmer of hope. While Jeremiah was still in prison, God gave him the following vision:

Thus said God: "In this place, which you say is in ruins, without a living soul—in the towns of Judah and the streets of Jerusalem that are desolate, without a person or animal, no inhabitants—there will once again be heard the sound of joy and gladness, the voice of the groom and bride, the voice of those who say, 'Give thanks to *Adonai Tz'vaot,* for God is good, God's kindness is eternal!' They will bring thanksgiving offerings to the Temple of God. I will restore their fortunes of the land as I did in the days of old."

JEREMIAH 33:10–11

Jeremiah was sad, and his writings expressed his sadness. But there is strength in his words, too. How can a person find strength in sadness?

_____

_____

Have you ever had a sad experience that made you a stronger person? Write about the experience and what it taught you.

_____

_____

_____

*In the next chapter, we will meet the last of the "Major Prophets," Ezekiel, who wrote much of his visionary writing while an exile in Babylon.*

# Chapter Seventeen

## EZEKIEL

*We have read the words and teachings of Elijah, Amos, Hosea, Isaiah, and Jeremiah. They all spoke out against corrupt kings and priests and warned about the bad things that would happen to people who disobeyed God. Ezekiel was a new kind of prophet. He wrote while he was in exile in Babylon. His messages were full of hope and promise, as well as strange mystical images.*

In 597 B.C.E., King Nebuchadnezzar of Babylon invaded Jerusalem. At that time a man named Ezekiel was deported—forced to move away from his country—to Babylon, along with King Jehoiachin and a large number of Judeans. According to his own writings, Ezekiel wrote from 593 until around 571 B.C.E., while living in Babylon.

Can you think of any person or group of people who have been forced from their homes in modern times? Perhaps one of your grandparents or great-grandparents came to this country as an exile. There might be students in your school who were forced out of their country because of their race or religion.

If you don't know of any, ask your parents or teachers for examples of modern exiles. Write a paragraph about one such case in the space below.

Imagine that your were exiled from your home. Imagine that you could only bring with you things that you could carry in a backpack.

| What would you bring with you? | After you had left your home, what would you miss the most? |
| --- | --- |
| | |

Ezekiel's writing came out of his experience as an exile. But his words are not angry political lectures, as many of the other prophets wrote. Ezekiel wrote about the holiness of God. In his sermons, he wrote about strange images, strange visions that he interprets as lessons from God.

Here are the opening chapters of the Book of **Ezekiel**:

In the thirtieth year, on the fifth day of the fourth month, when I was in the community of exiles by the Chebar Canal, the heavens opened up and I saw divine visions of God....

I looked and saw a stormy wind blowing from the north. A huge cloud was flashing fire, shining all around. At the center of the fire was a golden glow. There were four creatures there. This is how they looked:

Each had four faces and four wings. They had human hands beneath their wings. They all had faces and wings on all four of their sides. Because they had no front or back, they could move in all directions without having to turn.

Each had a human face in front, a lion's face on the right, an ox face on the left, and an eagle face at the back....

Something that looked like burning embers flashed like sparklers dashing to and fro between the creatures.

As I looked at the creatures, I saw a wheel on the ground by each of the four-faced creatures. Each of the wheels looked the same. They glimmered, and seemed to be made of two wheels each, spinning one inside the other.... The rims of the wheels were huge and had eyes all around them. Wherever the creatures went, the wheels went along with them. When they stopped, the wheels stopped. When they flew up, the wheels flew up. The spirit of the creatures was in these wheels.

High above the creatures stretched a crystal vault, and within its walls, the sound of the creatures' wings echoed like the sound of rushing waters, like the sound of the Almighty.

High above the vault was something that looked like a sapphire throne. Way up on the throne was a being that looked human, but with a body filled with glowing flame. There was light all around him, like a rainbow in the clouds. That is how the Presence of God appeared to me, and I threw myself flat on the ground.

It said, "Ben-Adam, stand up so that I can speak to you."

As It spoke, a spirit entered me and raised me to my feet.

It said, "Ben-Adam, I am sending you to the people of Israel, the nation that rebelled against me. You will go to them and tell them what God says. They may not listen, for they are very rebellious.

But they will know that a prophet was with them.

"And you, Ben-Adam, don't be afraid of them or of what they say to you, even if it bites like thistles, thorns, and scorpion stings.

"And Ben-Adam, don't be rebellious like those rebellious people. Open your mouth and eat what I give you."

I looked, and there was a hand stretching out to me holding a written scroll. As the hand unrolled it, I saw that written on both sides were lamentations, sad cries, and woes.

"Ben-Adam, eat what is given to you. Eat this scroll, and speak to the House of Israel."

So I opened my mouth.

"Ben-Adam, feed your stomach and fill your belly with this scroll that I give you."

I ate it, and it tasted as sweet as honey.

EZEKIEL 1:1, 4–10, 13–28; 2:1–3:3

To help us review Ezekiel's first prophecy, answer the following questions based on the above reading.

Where was Ezekiel when he had his vision?

_____

_____

God did not call Ezekiel by his own name, but called him a special name that means "son of man" or "human being." What was that name?

_____

In his vision, Ezekiel saw four creatures, each with four faces. What were the four faces?

_____

_____

_____

What did God ask Ezekiel to do at the end of the vision?

_____

_____

# Ezekiel's Vision

The opening chapters of Ezekiel contain several strange and mysterious visions. What are we supposed to make of the four-faced creatures or the being on the throne? Why did God call Ezekiel "Ben-Adam?" Why was Ezekiel commanded to eat the scroll?

Over the ages, scholars and rabbis have interpreted this vision in many ways. There are four main elements in the vision:

- The four creatures *(chayot)*
- The wheels *(ofanim)*
- The throne in the vault
- The being on the throne

In the space to the right, make a diagram showing—as best as you can estimate—what Ezekiel saw in his vision.

The Rabbis had a special name for the study of Ezekiel's vision. In the Talmud it is called *Maaseh Merkavah,* or the "Story of the Chariot." Can you guess why they called it "Chariot"?

_____

_____

Try your own hand at writing an explanation for the different things in Ezekiel's vision.

| WHEELS | CREATURES | THRONE | "BEING" |
|--------|-----------|--------|---------|
|        |           |        |         |

Can you think of an explanation for the four faces on the creatures? What do the eyes on the wheels represent?

| SYMBOL | MEANING |
|---|---|
| | |
| | |
| | |
| | |

The job of making interpretations—telling the meaning of symbols—is an important one for Jews and for anyone who studies the Bible. There are no right and wrong answers. Any answer that **makes sense** and **teaches** us something of value is a true interpretation.

# The Call of Ezekiel

In previous chapters, we have read about how God called on prophets and how the prophets didn't always want to listen.

The first unusual thing we notice about Ezekiel's calling is that God called him by an unusual name. "Ben-Adam" literally means "son of Adam" or "son of man." We often translate it as "human being." In the New Testament, Christian writers reinterpreted "Ben-Adam" as a reference to Jesus.

What do you think "Ben-Adam" means? Why did God call Ezekiel by this name? Why Ezekiel and not the other prophets before him? What special meaning might it have for Ezekiel?

_____

_____

Let's look again at God's message to Ezekiel, calling him to duty as a prophet:

> "Ben-Adam, I am sending you to the people of Israel, the nation that rebelled against me. You will go to them and tell them what God says. They may not listen, for they are very rebellious. But they will know that a prophet was with them.
>
> "And you, Ben-Adam, don't be afraid of them or of what they say to you, even if it bites like thistles, thorns, and scorpion stings."
>
> EZEKIEL 2:3–6

What did God command Ezekiel to do?

_____

What did God warn Ezekiel about?

_____

Explain God's words: "even if it bites like thistles, thorns, and scorpion stings." What was God referring to? Why did God use those images?

_____

_____

Next comes what may be the strangest part of Ezekiel's vision. God told the prophet: "Open your mouth and eat what I give you." What did God give to Ezekiel?

_____

_____

After Ezekiel ate what God handed him, how did it taste?

_____

_____

Can you explain this part of the vision? Why did God ask Ezekiel to eat it? What does it symbolize? What does it have to do with his job of speaking to the Israelites?

_____

_____

_____

# Ezekiel on God's Justice

Earlier prophets spoke angry messages to the people and their leaders, telling how furious God was with their sins. Like the other prophets, Ezekiel admitted that God would punish us for our misdeeds. But Ezekiel explained God's justice in a much more gentle manner. While the other prophets—and all people prior to Ezekiel, for that matter—felt that entire families, communities, or even nations would be destroyed for the sins of its leaders, Ezekiel said that God would punish only the person who sins.

Earlier prophets envisioned God burning with anger while giving punishment. When Ezekiel describes God's punishment, we see a sad, disappointed God, regretting the task of punishment but knowing that it is necessary.

In the eighteenth chapter of Ezekiel, the prophet proclaimed God's message about justice:

If a person is righteous...and has not done anything wrong, if he has been truly fair between man and man, if he has followed My laws and kept My rules and acted honestly, that person shall live!...

The person who sins, that person alone shall die! A child shall not be punished for a parent's guilt. A parent shall not be punished for a child's guilt. The good deeds of the good shall be credited to the good alone. The wickedness of the wicked shall be accounted to the wicked alone.

If a wicked person turns away from all the sins he had committed and keeps all My laws and does what is just and right, he shall live. He shall not die. None of the sins he committed shall be held against him. Because of the righteousness he practices, he shall live.

I don't want a wicked person to die! I want him to turn back from his ways and live!...

Some people say that God is not fair.

Listen House of Israel, it is not God that is unfair. It is your ways that are unfair. You can be certain, House of Israel, that I will judge each of you according to what you have done. Your sins do not need to be a stumbling block of guilt for you. Cast away all your sins and get yourself a new heart and a new spirit so that you won't die, House of Israel.

I do not want anyone to die, declares God. Therefore, repent and live!

EZEKIEL 18:5, 8–9, 20–23, 29–32

Imagine that Ezekiel has asked your public relations firm to develop an advertising campaign—a public service announcement—that will encourage people to act in a fair and righteous way. In the space below, design a poster or billboard that uses words from Ezekiel, along with whatever images you choose, to help promote Ezekiel's campaign.

How fair/unfair was Ezekiel's message about God's justice? Summarize Ezekiel's message in the space below.

_____

_____

_____

_____

# Dry Bones

Perhaps the most famous of Ezekiel's visions is his prophecy of the valley of dry bones. It is a powerful image both literally and as a symbol or metaphor for something else.

The hand of God came upon me and took me by the spirit of God to a valley. If was full of bones. God led me all around them. There were many of them, spread all over the valley, and they were very dry.

God said to me, "Ben-Adam, can these bones live again?"

I answered, "O God, only You know."

God said to me, "Prophesy over these bones. Tell them, 'Dry bones, hear the word of God. I will cause breath to enter you, and you shall live again. I will place muscles on you and cover you with flesh. I will form skin over you. And I will put breath into you, and you will live again. And you shall know that I am God.'"

I prophesied as I had been commanded. While I was speaking, suddenly there was a sound of rattling. The bones came together, bone connecting with bone. I saw muscles on them, and then flesh had grown and skin was forming. But they had no breath yet.

God said, "Prophesy for breath, Ben-Adam. Tell the breath, 'Come from the four winds, breath, and breathe into these bodies so that they may live again.'"

I prophesied as God had commanded me, and they came to life, getting up on their feet. There were many of them.

God said to me, "Ben-Adam, these bones are the entire people of Israel. They have been saying, 'Our bones are dried up, our hope is gone, we are doomed.' You shall prophesy to them saying, 'God is going to open your graves, lift you up, and bring you back to the land of Israel. You will know that God has spoken when you have been filled with breath and brought to your own land.'"

EZEKIEL 37:1–14

What did Ezekiel see in the valley? Recap his vision in your own words.

_____

_____

_____

How do you think you would react if you saw what Ezekiel saw?

_____

_____

Ezekiel's vision has inspired several songs, including this popular African-American spiritual:

## Dry Bones

*Ezekiel cried, "Dem dry bones!"*
*Ezekiel cried, "Dem dry bones!"*
*Ezekiel cried, "Dem dry bones!"*
*"Oh, hear the word of the Lord."*

*The foot bone connected to the leg bone,*
*The leg bone connected to the knee bone,*
*The knee bone connected to the thigh bone,*
*The thigh bone connected to the back bone,*
*The back bone connected to the neck bone,*
*The neck bone connected to the head bone,*
*Oh, hear the word of the Lord!*

*Dem bones, dem bones gonna walk aroun'*
*Dem bones, dem bones, gonna walk aroun'*

*Dem bones, dem bones, gonna walk aroun'*
*Oh, hear the word of the Lord.*

*The head bone connected to the neck bone,*
*The neck bone connected to the back bone,*
*The back bone connected to the thigh bone,*
*The thigh bone connected to the knee bone,*
*The knee bone connected to the leg bone,*
*The leg bone connected to the foot bone,*
*Oh, hear the word of the Lord!*

Why do you think the story of the valley of dry bones was so popular among African-American slaves in the nineteenth century?

_____

_____

God explained the meaning of the dry bones to Ezekiel:

> "Ben-Adam, these bones are the entire people of Israel. They have been saying, 'Our bones are dried up, our hope is gone, we are doomed.'"
>
> EZEKIEL 37:11

Why did God compare the people of Israel to a valley of dry bones?

_____

_____

If the dry bones are the people of Israel, then what is the meaning of the bones coming together, growing flesh, and rising?

_____

_____

Imagine that the hope of Jews today has gone dry. Imagine that our connection with God and with each other has become brittle. How could Ezekiel's message help us to rise again?

_____

_____

_In this chapter, we learned about Ezekiel, a prophet who lived and wrote during the early part of the Babylonian exile. His message was one of hope and of mysterious visions. In the next chapter, we will meet another prophet who continued Ezekiel's tradition with visions of hope and of Israel's return from exile._

# Chapter Eighteen

# ZECHARIAH AND ISRAEL'S RETURN

*The Book of **Ezekiel** contains the famous vision of the bones rising in the desert. In this chapter, we will read of how that prophecy was fulfilled when the people of Judah, exiled for fifty years in Babylon, returned to their land. Like **Ezekiel**, the Book of **Zechariah** is full of mysterious visions and images. Zechariah's visions were strong and positive promises that Ezekiel's message of hope would soon come to pass.*

So far, we have looked at the writings of the prophets Amos, Hosea, Isaiah, Jeremiah, and Ezekiel. These prophets lived and wrote from the middle of the eighth century B.C.E. through the Babylonian exile, in the middle of the sixth century B.C.E.

To review major historical events of the time and how the prophets fit into those times, look at the table below.

| TIMELINE OF THE LITERARY PROPHETS | |
|---|---|
| 933 B.C.E. | **Death of King Solomon; the kingdom split into Israel and Judah** |
| 873–843 | Elijah active as a prophet |
| ~760 | Amos begins prophesying |
| ~750 | Hosea |
| ~740 | Isaiah |
| ~725 | Micah |
| 722 | **Israel destroyed by Assyria** |
| 630 | Zephaniah |
| 626–586 | Jeremiah |
| ~615 | Nahum |
| 605 | Habakkuk |
| 597 | **First Babylonian exile** |
| ~593–571 | Ezekiel |
| 586 | **Nebuchadnezzar conquers Jerusalem; second Babylonian exile** |
| ~540 | Second Isaiah |
| 538 | **Cyrus ushers Jews back to Judea; end of Babylonian exile** |
| ~520 | Haggai and Zechariah |
| ~500 | Obadiah |
| ~460 | Malachi |
| 400 | Joel |
| 300 | Book of **Jonah** written (~300–250 B.C.E.) |

To help review the prophets and the events that they lived through, this era of Jewish history has been divided into four periods: (1) the period of the two kingdoms; (2) the pre-exile years; (3) the Babylonian exile; and (4) the post-exile years. Using the timeline of the Literary Prophets on page 171 as your guide, copy the names of all the prophets listed below into the appropriate time period.

| Two Kingdoms | Pre-Exile Years | Babylonian Exile | Post-Exile Years |
|---|---|---|---|
| (933–722 B.C.E.) | (722–587 B.C.E.) | (597–538 B.C.E.) | (538–250 B.C.E.) |
| | | | |

**Prophets**

| | | | |
|---|---|---|---|
| Amos | Ezekiel | Habakkuk | Haggai | Hosea |
| Isaiah | Jeremiah | Jonah | Micah | Nahum |
| Second Isaiah* | Zechariah | Zephaniah | | |

* Second Isaiah—sometimes called Deutero-Isaiah—was the person who wrote some of the later chapters of the Book of **Isaiah.** We don't know who he was or even if his name was Isaiah. But since his writings were added to the writings of Isaiah, we call him Second Isaiah.

# Return from Exile

Zechariah began writing his prophecies around the year 520 B.C.E. He lived through the end of the Babylonian exile and saw the return of the exiled people of Judah to their homes.

Sixteen years passed. The Kingdom of Judah was rebuilt, but the Jewish people had not rebuilt the Temple, which was destroyed by the Babylonians in 586 B.C.E. Two prophets from this period, Haggai and Zechariah, urged the leaders of Judah to begin building a new Temple in Jerusalem. Why do you think a Temple was important to them? What religious activities could not be done without the Temple?

_____

_____

_____

The following text contains the opening verses of the Book of **Zechariah.** Darius, who is mentioned at the beginning of the text, was the king of Persia. He came to the throne after the death of Cambyses, the son and successor of Cyrus, the Persian ruler who defeated the Babylonians and helped the Jews return from exile.

In the eighth month of the second year of Darius, this word of God came to the prophet Zechariah son of Berechiah:

God was angry with your ancestors. Turn back to Me, and I will turn back to you. Do not be like your ancestors. When the earlier prophets told them to turn back from their evil ways and evil deeds, they did not listen or obey Me. Where are your ancestors now? Did the prophets live forever? These warnings outlived them all. In the end they all had to admit that God dealt with them according to their actions.

ZECHARIAH 1:1–6

According to Zechariah, why was God angry with their ancestors?

_____

_____

The text ends with the statement "God dealt with them according to their actions." What did Zechariah mean by this? What were their actions? How did God deal with them?

_____

_____

The Book of **Zechariah,** like the Book of **Isaiah,** contains sections that were actually written by the prophet together with other writings that were written by some unknown author much later. There are fourteen chapters in the Book of **Zechariah;** the first eight chapters were written by Zechariah, and the final six chapters were written sometime around 300 B.C.E., more than 200 years later.

The prophecies of Zechariah, found in the first half of the book, include eight visions that tell of Israel's return from exile and of their new leader, Zerubbabel. In each vision, the prophet saw a different image or scene. Each image represented some event or idea that would help rebuild the Temple and the Kingdom of Judah.

The visions all took place at night. Try to imagine the man sitting by a fire, at the side of a mountain, 2,500 years ago. Just as he was nodding off to sleep, he was startled by something he saw or thought he saw.

Unlike the earlier prophets, who never mentioned interpreting angels, Zechariah regularly referred to someone—a man or an angel—who helped him interpret his visions. Each time he was shown something new: four horses, an altar with sharp horns, a menorah, and an olive tree. When he asked what the objects mean, the man or angel answered him.

Putting yourself in Zechariah's place, what would it feel like to have a vision like this? Would you be startled? Scared? Unsure if you are dreaming or actually seeing something real?

_____

_____

_____

In this chapter, we will look at four of the eight visions, starting with the first—the vision of the four horses.

## The First Vision

In the night, I had a vision: I saw a man mounted on a red horse, standing among the myrtle trees in the field. Behind him were another red horse, a black horse, and a white horse.

I asked, "What are these, sir?" and the angel who talked with me said, "I will tell you."

Then the man who was standing among the myrtle trees spoke up and said, "They were sent out by God to roam the earth."

And then they told the angel, "We have roamed the earth, and everything is now peaceful."

Then the angel said, "Oh God, how long before you forgive Jerusalem and the towns of Judah, which you cursed seventy years ago?"

Then God answered with kind, gentle words to the angel who was talking with me.

Then the angel said, "This is what God says: 'I am very protective of Jerusalem. The other nations punished them, but they went too far. Now my favor returns to Jerusalem. My House will be built there. A measuring line will be stretched out over Jerusalem. My towns will overflow with plenty. God will again comfort Zion and choose Jerusalem again.'"

ZECHARIAH 1:8–17

Describe what Zechariah saw in this vision.

_____

_____

What did the horses say to Zechariah and the angel?

_____

_____

What would you say is the purpose of this prophecy? Is it meant to warn the people?
To comfort them? To tell them to change their ways?

_____

_____

# The Second Vision

Zechariah's second vision involved four horns. The text doesn't tell us what kind of
horns they were, or if they were attached to anything. Perhaps they were the sharp pro-
truding horns on an altar used for sacrifices. They may also have represented the four
winds, or four corners of the world. Also in this vision were four smiths, metalworkers
who usually make tools or weapons. Here is the second vision:

I looked up and saw four sharp horns. I asked the angel who was talking with me, "What are those?"

He answered, "Those are the horns that tossed Judah, Israel, and Jerusalem."

Then God showed me four smiths.

"What are they going to do?" I asked.

He answered, "These men are coming to frighten them and cut down the horns of the nations who raised their points against Judah and scattered it."

ZECHARIAH 2:1–4

When Zechariah asked the angel what the horns mean, the angel answered, "Those are
the horns that tossed Judah, Israel, and Jerusalem." What do you think he meant by
that?

_____

_____

The smiths came to "frighten them" and "cut down the horns." Whom did they come to frighten: the Jews or their enemies?

_____

_____

Why were the smiths cutting down the horns?

_____

_____

# The Third Vision

In the third vision, Zechariah saw a young man with a measuring tape:

> I looked up and saw a man holding a measuring tape. I asked, "Where are you going?" and he said, "To measure Jerusalem to see how long and wide it will be." Another angel came and said to the angel who was talking with me, "Go tell that young man that Jerusalem will be full of people like a city with no walls to limit it, and God says, 'I will be a wall of fire all around it, and I will be the glory inside it.'"
>
> ZECHARIAH 2:5–9

What was the man measuring?

_____

What did the angel tell the man?

_____

_____

The Rabbis of the Talmud enjoyed analyzing details of the stories in the *Tanakh*. When they studied the Book of **Zechariah**, one of the questions that they asked themselves was why Jerusalem needed to be measured. The following midrash, found in the *Bava Batra* section of the Babylonian Talmud, answers the question by turning two lines from the text into a story:

Rabbi Chanina bar Papa said: The Holy One wished to confine Jerusalem within specific measurements, for it is said, "I asked, 'Where are you going?' and he said, 'To measure Jerusalem to see how long and wide it will be'" (Zechariah 2:6). But one of the angels said to the Holy One, "Master of the Universe, You have created in Your world many cities for the nations of the earth, but You did not set the measure of their length or width. Why then are You fixing the measurements of Jerusalem, the city in which Your Name, Your Sanctuary, and Your righteous dwell?" Then one angel said to another, "Go tell that young man that Jerusalem will be full of people like a city with no walls to limit it" (Zechariah 2:8.)

According to Rabbi Chanina bar Papa, why was Jerusalem being measured?

_____

_____

Why did the angel at the end of the midrash say, "Jerusalem will be full of people like a city with no walls to limit it"?

_____

_____

# The Fifth Vision

Now we'll look at Zechariah's fifth vision, which is one of the most memorable images in the Book of **Zechariah.**

The text mentions a man who was a very important political figure during the time of Zechariah. Zerubbabel was a descendant of King David and was the grandson of King Jehoiachin. There was not a new king over Judah, but King Darius of Persia appointed Zerubbabel as the governor of the region.

Because Zerubbabel was a descendant of David, many Jews during that time hoped that Zerubbabel would be a strong and glorious king like David had been nearly five hundred years earlier. People of the time spoke about a dream of a "new anointed one" who would be the "seed of David." It is from this hope that the idea of a Messiah (anointed one) developed.

Now read the text of the Zechariah's fifth vision:

An angel came to me and woke me as one is wakened from sleep. He said to me, "What do you see?"

I answered, "I see a menorah, all of gold, with a bowl above it. It has seven lamps on it, and the bowl above it has seven pipes. There are two olive trees beside it, one on the right of the bowl and one on its left. What do those things mean?" I asked the angel.

He explained to me as follows:

"This is the word of God to Zerubbabel:

'Not by might,

And not by power,

But by My spirit.

Great mountains will flatten in the path of Zerubbabel.

He will take out a great stone,

They will all shout, Beautiful! Beautiful!

Zerubbabel's hands have begun this Temple

And Zerubbabel's hands will complete it.

No one should mock these small beginnings.

When they see the stone in Zerubbabel's hand they will rejoice.

Those seven lights are the eyes of God, covering the entire earth.'"

"And what," I asked, "are those two olive trees? And what are those things on top of the trees bringing oil through golden tubes?"

"They are the two anointed ones—priest and king—standing before the God of all earth."

ZECHARIAH 4:1–14

The two important symbols in this vision were the menorah and the olive trees. According to the angel, what was the meaning of the lights of the menorah?

_____

_____

And what was the meaning of the two olive trees? Whom did the trees represent?

_____

_____

Israel had no king at that time. Instead, Zerubbabel was their political leader. The High Priest then was a man named Joshua. Why would Zechariah's vision suggest that these two men were God's anointed ones? Is it important that there are two of them?

_____

_____

_____

# Coming of a Messianic King

As we read earlier in this chapter, the Jewish people were hoping that the kingdom would be restored and that a king like King David would unite the people once again. Kings were anointed with oil. The Hebrew word for "anointed" is *mashiach*.

Many of the prophets wrote about their hope for the coming of an anointed descendant of David, *mashiach ben David*. As time wore on, the idea of a *mashiach* מָשִׁיחַ (or "messiah" in English) grew into something more than just a political leader. Particularly for the prophets who came after Zechariah and Haggai, the coming of the Messiah meant that the whole world would be united under God and the world and nature would be at peace.

The second half of the Book of **Zechariah** contains poems and visions by a man who lived much later than Zechariah himself. These chapters, written around 300 B.C.E., two hundred years or more after the time of Zechariah's own writing, reflect the new meaning of "Messiah."

> The day of God is coming when all that has been taken from you will be returned....
>
> On that day, there will be no cold, no frost. It will be a continuous day with neither day nor night, but will always be light.
>
> On that day, fresh water will flow from Jerusalem, flowing to the Dead Sea and to the Mediterranean Sea all summer and winter.
>
> And God shall be ruler over all the earth. On that day, *Adonai* will be one and God's name will be one.
>
> Jerusalem will be raised high in her place. Never again shall there be destruction, and Jerusalem will be safe.
>
> ZECHARIAH 14:1, 6–11

Using the images from the text on the previous page, design a poster showing what life will be like during the time of the Messiah.

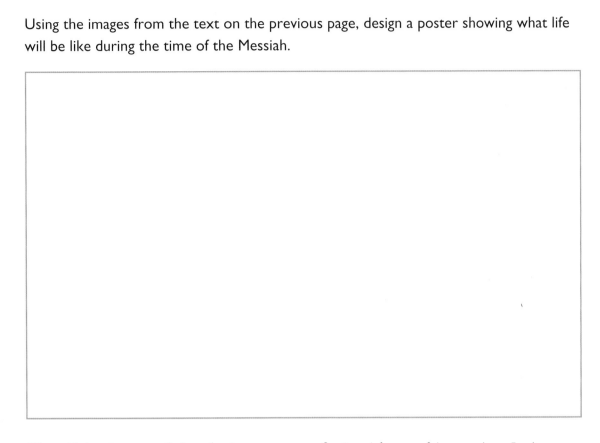

The *Aleinu* is one of the closing prayers of a Jewish worship service. In it, we are reminded that it is our duty to praise God. The *Aleinu* ends with a passage about a messianic future in which God will rule over all things:

וְנֶאֱמַר: וְהָיָה יְיָ מֶלֶךְ עַל־כָּל־הָאָרֶץ
בַּיּוֹם הַהוּא יִהְיֶה יְיָ אֶחָד וּשְׁמוֹ אֶחָד

The word of your prophet (will be) fulfilled: "The Eternal God will reign forever and ever. On that day, O God, You shall be One and Your name shall be One."

Find and underline the verses from the Zechariah text that were the source for these lines from the *Aleinu.*

*In this chapter, we reviewed the Literary Prophets and looked closely at the visions of Zechariah. We also learned how the idea of "Messiah" grew from a political leader into something almost superhuman. In chapter 19, we will take a look at the last of our Literary Prophets with the Book of **Jonah**.*

# Chapter Nineteen

## JONAH

*The story of "Jonah and the Whale" may have been one of the first Bible stories you ever heard. The story of Jonah is much more than a children's story. Each year, the Book of **Jonah** is read as the haftarah portion during the Yom Kippur Afternoon Service. Did you know that the text never says that it was a whale that swallowed Jonah? It was a big fish. In this chapter, we will learn about the lessons taught in the Book of **Jonah**.*

The last of the Twelve Prophets is very different from the other Literary Prophets. Instead of speeches or prophecies written by the prophet, the Book of **Jonah** tells a story, in four chapters, about a prophet who doesn't want to do his job.

Can you match the prophets with the jobs God called on them to do?

| | |
|---|---|
| Joshua | "Ben-Adam, eat what is given to you. Eat this scroll, and speak to the House of Israel." |
| Samuel | "I am sending you to Pharaoh, in order to bring the Israelites out of Egypt." |
| Elijah | "Now it is time for you and all these people to cross the Jordan into the land that I am giving them." |
| Ezekiel | "Listen to [the people's] demands. Give them a king." |
| Moses | "Go down and confront King Ahab of Israel who lives in Samaria. Tell him, 'The very place where the dogs lapped up Naboth's blood, the dogs will lap up your blood as well.'" |

The Hebrew prophets were called by God to serve, lead, and speak to the Jewish people. Jonah was different. God called on Jonah to speak to a non-Jewish nation. Jonah was told to go to the people of the Assyrian city of Nineveh and to tell the people there to change their ways.

But Jonah had no interest in helping the Assyrians. He would help the Israelites, but he wanted nothing to do with the other nations. He would be perfectly happy if God wiped Nineveh off the face of the earth.

The Book of **Jonah** was written around 300 B.C.E. It is one of the last prophetic books to have been written. Unlike the other prophetic books, which contain historical material and prophecies, Jonah is a story. It is probably a work of fiction. The author of **Jonah** created the story in order to teach a Jewish lesson.

At the time that the Book of **Jonah** was written, many Jews disagreed about whether Jews should share their religious ideas with non-Jews. There were good reasons on both sides of the debate. In the boxes below, write down three reasons why Jews should cooperate with the non-Jewish nations, and three reasons why the Jews should keep to themselves.

| Jews should cooperate, interact, and share religious ideas with non-Jewish people. | Jews should keep to themselves as much as possible and not try to teach their beliefs to non-Jews. |
|---|---|
| 1._____ _____ | 1._____ _____ |
| 2._____ _____ | 2._____ _____ |
| 3._____ _____ | 3._____ _____ |

According to the story, God had no desire to destroy. The writers of the books of *N'vi-im* believed that God wanted all people of all nations to turn to God. As we learned in the chapter about Ezekiel, God said, "I don't want a wicked person to die! I want him to turn back from his ways and live!" (Ezekiel 18:23).

Instead of doing his mission and helping the people of Nineveh to repent, Jonah thought he could avoid his duty by running away to Tarshish, a distant city whose location is not known to us today.

Here is the story of the prophet Jonah and what God called on him to do:

The word of God came to Jonah, son of Amittai: "Go at once to Nineveh, that great city, and tell them that I know of their wickedness."

Jonah, however, fled to Tarshish to escape from God. At Jaffa he found a ship leaving for Tarshish. He bought passage and went aboard to sail to Tarshish.

But God blew a powerful wind on the sea, and a great storm nearly destroyed the ship. The frightened sailors cried out, each praying to their own gods, and began throwing cargo overboard to make the ship lighter.

But through all this, Jonah had gone to sleep below deck. When the captain found out, he awakened him, yelling, "How can you sleep? Get up and pray to your god! Maybe your god will have mercy and not let us drown."

The men cast lots to find out who was responsible for the disaster. The lot fell on Jonah. They said to him, "All right, you, who brought this misfortune on us, what is your business? Where is your country? What people do you come from?"

"I am a Hebrew," he answered. "I worship *Adonai*, the God of Heaven, who made the earth and the sea."

This frightened the men. They asked, "What have you done?" When they learned that he was trying to escape God, they asked, "What can we do to stop the storm?"

"Throw me overboard," he said. "The sea will calm down. I know that this terrible storm happened because of me."

The men tried to keep the ship afloat. But the sea grew more and more stormy. Finally they cried, "Please God, we don't want to die because of this man. But don't hold us guilty of killing an innocent man."

They threw him overboard, and the sea settled. In great respect for God, the men offered a sacrifice.

JONAH 1:1–16

In the text you just read, God called on Jonah. What did God ask him to do?

_____

The sailors aboard Jonah's ship were not Jews. How do we know this from reading the text?

_____    _____

_____

Why did the sailors think Jonah caused the storm?

_____

_____

# Jonah's Mission

God called on Jonah for a very special task. Jonah was not the first prophet called on to take God's message to non-Jewish nations. In fact, at some point in the careers of nearly all the prophets, they were called on to prophesy to the "nations."

In chapter 49 of **Isaiah**, God told the Israelites:

> I will make you a light to the nations,
> So that My salvation will reach to the ends
> of the earth.
>
> ISAIAH 49:6

The Hebrew *l'or goyim* לְאוֹר גּוֹיִים means "light to the nations." Over the years, Jewish people have referred to people of non-Jewish communities as "the nations" or "goyim." In the Bible, this was a neutral term simply meaning "gentiles" or "non-Jews." But as time went on, Jews often used the words "goyim" or "goy" as negative or insulting words to label non-Jews.

Jewish tradition teaches us to be proud of our religion and our people. Is it necessary to insult non-Jewish nations in order to be proud of our own? What do you think?

_____

_____

_____

Unfortunately for Jonah, he thought of the "nations" in a negative way. He felt that as a Jew he was better than them and that they didn't deserve God's message. God didn't agree.

# The Drawing of Lots

The drawing of lots seems like a very unusual custom to modern readers. In order to find out who was responsible for the storm, the sailors used things called *goralot*. As best as we can determine, *goralot* were stones or markers that were placed in a bag or container. When the container was shaken, the first stone to come out provided the answer.

*Goralot,* or lots, were used to answer questions, to select volunteers, and to determine guilt or distinction. Ancient peoples believed that a divinity might communicate a direct answer to them through the stones.

Do we have anything like lots in the modern world? What about the game "Eeny-Meeny-Miney-Mo" that children use to choose whose turn is next? Or have you seen the toy Magic 8 Ball? It's a plastic ball filled with water, with a twenty-sided die inside. As a game, people shake the ball, ask it a question, and look for the answer to appear in the window.

Can you think of any other forms of *goralot* that modern people use? What tricks, toys, or games have you used to help make a decision?

_____

_____

Generally, the writers of the Bible frown on some activities of this type. The activities of which they disapprove are in the category of "divination." Using objects to guess the future is called "divining" and is considered a sin. However, there were objects called Urim and Thummim that were used by priests in the Temple as a source of divine messages and were considered legitimate.

As the story of Jonah continues, an amazing event occurred:

God designated a huge fish that swallowed Jonah. Jonah stayed in the belly of the fish for three days and nights and prayed to God....

Then God commanded the fish to spew Jonah out onto dry land.

The word of God came to Jonah again. "Go at once to Nineveh, the great city, and proclaim to them what I tell you."

Jonah did as God commanded.

Nineveh was a huge city. It took three days to walk from one end to the other. Jonah made his way to the city and announced, "In forty days, Nineveh will be overthrown!"

The people of Nineveh believed in God. They fasted and put on sackcloth. When the king of Nineveh heard, he too put on sackcloth and sat in ashes. He proclaimed, "No one, human or animal, may eat or drink. You shall wear sackcloth and cry out to God. Everyone shall turn from their evil ways and injustices. Perhaps God, too, will turn from his anger and let us live."

When God saw how they were turning from their evil ways, God took back the punishment planned for them.

JONAH 2:1–2, 11; 3:1–10

Jonah did as God had told him. He went to the people of Nineveh and was a "light to the nations"—*l'or goyim*. Even though he didn't want to help the people of Nineveh, it appears that he did a good job prophesying to them. How can we tell that Jonah was successful?

_____

_____

Jonah had mixed feelings about his success. As we see in this next text, Jonah still had a lesson to learn. God used an example of a gourd plant to teach him that God is the God of all nations.

Jonah was very unhappy about this. He prayed to God, saying, "This is exactly what I said would happen when I was back home. That's why I ran off to Tarshish. I know that You are a compassionate and forgiving God, slow in anger, full of kindness, taking away punishment. Please, God, kill me. I would rather be dead than alive."

Jonah went off to a place east of the city. He set up a camp where he could watch what was happening in the city. God made a gourd plant grow up over Jonah to give him extra shade and protection. He was very happy about the plant until the next morning, when God had a worm attack the gourd so that it withered. As the sun rose, God sent a hot east wind to beat down on Jonah's head until he felt faint. He begged for death.

God said, "Are you depressed because of what happened to the plant?"

Jonah answered, "Yes, so much that I want to die."

God said, "You cared about the plant, even though you had spent no time or energy taking care of it. And you say that I shouldn't care for a great city like Nineveh, with more than 120,000 inhabitants—people who don't know right from left?"

JONAH 4:1–11

Just as Jonah didn't understand God's purpose in prophesying to the people of Nineveh, sometimes we don't like the things that our parents or teachers ask us to do.

Can you think of a time when you were told to do something that you didn't want to do? Something that you didn't understand at the time? How did it make you feel? Were you angry or upset like Jonah?

_____

_____

In time, we usually grow to understand the reasons for the tasks we are told to do. Look at the example that you wrote above. Seeing it from the point of view of your parent or teacher, there was a good reason for making you do it. Can you describe that below?

_____

_____

We read the Book of **Jonah** each year as the haftarah portion for Yom Kippur afternoon. During Yom Kippur, we are told to atone and apologize for our mistakes, to fast from eating and drinking, and to do *t'shuvah* תְּשׁוּבָה—repentance.

**What lessons for Yom Kippur can we learn from the Book of Jonah?**

_____

_____

What we are most likely to remember about the story of Jonah is the giant fish that swallowed him out at sea. We must also keep in mind the values that are presented in the Book of **Jonah:** that it is possible for any person of any nation or religion to turn toward God, and that we cannot run away from our responsibilities.

*In this chapter, we read the Book of* **Jonah**. *Just as Jonah is unusual among the prophets, the Book of* **Jonah** *is unique among the prophetic books. Most of the books of N'vi-im contain histories or prophetic speeches. Jonah reads more like a story or fable. In the next several chapters, we will be reading other books of the* Tanakh *that teach us lessons using stories or poetry. These next Bible books come from the third section of the* Tanakh, K'tuvim.

# Chapter Twenty

## PSALMS AND PROVERBS

*In the previous chapter, we read the Book of **Jonah**, a book that teaches Jewish values by means of a story. Beginning with this chapter, we will be looking at the third and final set of books from the Tanakh: the Writings, or K'tuvim. Some of the K'tuvim contain lesson stories similar to the Book of **Jonah**. Others are books of poetry and value lessons, as in the two books we will examine in this chapter, **Psalms** and **Proverbs**.*

# K'tuvim

After the Torah and *N'vi-im*, the final grouping of books in the *Tanakh* is *K'tuvim* כְּתוּבִים, Writings. There are eleven books in *K'tuvim*, although in modern Bibles two of the books are divided in half, making a total of thirteen books. (**Ezra-Nehemiah,** which was originally one book, became two separate books in later translations, and Chronicles was divided into **First Chronicles** and **Second Chronicles.**)

Here are the names of the eleven books in English and Hebrew, along with a short description of each book. Five of the books are also marked as part of the five *m'gillot*.

---

**Psalms** (T'hilim תְּהִלִּים)—150 poems to and about God

**Proverbs** (Mishlei מִשְׁלֵי)—poems that teach instructions on how to be a good person

**Job** (Iyov אִיּוֹב)—a story made up of poems that helps us think about why bad things happen to good people

**Song of Songs** (Shir HaShirim שִׁיר הַשִׁירִים)—poems of love; *m'gillah* for Pesach

**Ruth** (Rut רוּת)—the story of a brave woman who joins the Jewish people; *m'gillah* for Shavuot

**Lamentations** (Eichah אֵיכָה)—five poems of sadness about the Babylonian exile; *m'gillah* for Tishah B'Av

**Ecclesiastes** (Kohelet קֹהֶלֶת)—a discussion of how we can find happiness with some poems; *m'gillah* for Sukkot

**Esther** (Ester אֶסְתֵּר)—the story of a Jewish woman who saved her people from an evil Persian politician; *m'gillah* for Purim

**Daniel** (Daniyeil דָּנִיֵּאל)—adventures of a young man living during and after the Babylonian exile

**Ezra-Nehemiah** (Ezra-N'chemyah עֶזְרָא-נְחֶמְיָה)—history of the return of the Jews to Jerusalem after the Babylonian exile and the rebuilding of the nation

**Chronicles** (Divrei HaYamim דִּבְרֵי הַיָּמִים)—"The Book of Daily Matters"; history of the Jews from the time of Creation until King Cyrus of Persia returns the Jews to Jerusalem

---

What kinds of books are found in *K'tuvim?* We can catagorize them in several ways. In the boxes below, copy the names of all the books that fit the category. Be sure to read the descriptions of each book carefully in order to discover where to place them. Remember: most of the books belong to more than one category, and it isn't necessary to fill all the spaces provided.

## BOOKS OF POETRY

1._____
2._____
3._____
4._____
5._____
6._____

## BOOKS OF HISTORY

1._____
2._____
3._____
4._____
5._____
6._____

## STORIES

1._____
2._____
3._____
4._____
5._____
6._____

## LESSON BOOKS

1._____
2._____
3._____
4._____
5._____
6._____

## THE *M'GILLOT*

1._____
2._____
3._____
4._____
5._____

# Hebrew Poetry—A Review

In chapter 12, we learned about some of the characteristics of Hebrew poetry. We learned that verses usually come in pairs, called couplets.

We learned that the verses in a couplet usually have the same number of beats.

We also learned that poetry is filled with mood and image. Poems do not need to describe something in detail, and they aren't concerned with getting the facts exactly right. Instead, poetry tries to get the reader to feel and see things that are sometimes hard to describe with words.

Image is especially important in the poetry we will find in the *K'tuvim* books of the *Tanakh*. In the **Psalms, Proverbs,** and **Song of Songs,** the Torah can be a tree or a lamp or a crown on your head. A person can be a gazelle or a stag. Whenever we read a verse of poetry, we should ask ourselves what the images make us think about.

The last characteristic of poetry, and especially in Hebrew poetry, is parallelism. When the two lines of a couplet say similar things—or sometimes opposite things—the words of one line can usually be matched with the words of the next line.

For example, in the next section we will look at some verses from **Psalms.** Here are a few of the parallel couplets that we'll be reading. For both couplets, draw lines connecting the parallel words, and in the space provided, describe what makes them parallel.

| | |
|---|---|
| Shout for joy to God, all the earth!<br><br><br><br>Worship God with gladness, | |
| Enter God's gates with praise,<br><br><br><br>God's courts with admiration. | |

# Psalms

The Book of **Psalms** (*T'hilim* תְּהִילִים in Hebrew) is a collection of 150 poems. The word *"t'hilim"* means "praises" and comes from the same root as the word "Hallelujah," which means "praise God."

The word "psalms" comes from a Greek word meaning "a song sung to a stringed instrument." These poems were once part of a musical tradition. During the time of the Second Temple, they were read as part of the sacrificial services.

The psalms are poems that praise God, ask for things from God, and contemplate the nature of God. The prayerbook is filled with psalms, including the following two, which appear in the traditional weekday Morning Service:

*Shout for joy to God, all the earth!*
*Worship God with gladness,*
*Come in God's presence with shouts of joy.*
*Know that Adonai is God,*
*It is God who made us, we are God's,*
*God's people, the flock God tends.*
*Enter God's gates with praise,*
*God's courts with admiration.*
*Praise God!*
*Bless God's name!*
*For God is good,*

*God's love is everlasting,*
*God's faithfulness is for all generations.*

PSALM 100

*Sing unto God a new song,*
*Sing unto God, all the earth.*
*Sing unto God, bless God's name*
*Proclaim God's victory day after day.*
*Tell of God's glory among the nations,*
*God's wondrous deeds, among all peoples.*

PSALM 96:1–3

What do you think is the purpose of these psalms? Are they meant to make the reader happy? Sad? Angry? Relaxed? Excited? What do you think?

_____

_____

Both of the above psalms are read toward the beginning of the Morning Service. Why do you think they were placed there?

_____

_____

# The Twenty-Third Psalm

The most famous of the psalms is the Twenty-Third Psalm. Jews and Christians often read this psalm at funerals and memorial services. It reminds us that even when terrible things happen in our lives, God is there to give us comfort.

Below are two different translations of Psalm 23. The first one is a modern translation. The second is a more traditional translation. The language and style of the second are more old-fashioned, and it is more familiar to most people in that form.

*God is my shepherd,*
*I have all that I need.*
*God makes me rest in green pastures*
*Leads me to still waters;*
*Renews my life;*
*Guides me in right paths*
*According to God's name.*
*Though I walk through the valley of the*
  *shadow of death,*
*I fear no harm,*
*for You are with me;*
*Your rod and your staff*
*comfort me.*
*You spread a table for me in full view of*
  *my enemies;*
*You anoint my head with oil;*
*My cup overflows.*
*Goodness and love follow me all the days*
  *of my life,*
*And I shall live in the House of God forever.*
                    PSALM 23

*The Lord is my shepherd,*
*I shall not want;*
*He makes me lie down in green pastures.*
*He leads me beside still waters;*
*He restores my soul.*

*He leads me in paths of righteousness*
*For His name's sake.*
*Yea, though I walk through the valley of*
  *the shadow of death,*
*I fear no evil;*
*For you are with me,*
*Thy rod and thy staff,*
*They comfort me.*
*Thou preparest a table before me*
*In the presence of mine enemies;*
*Thou anointest my head with oil,*
*My cup overflows.*
*Surely goodness and mercy shall follow me*
  *all the days of my life;*
*And I shall dwell in the House of the Lord*
  *forever.*
                    PSALM 23

God is called a shepherd at the beginning of this psalm. Of course, we know that God is not a shepherd. The poet is using the **image** of a shepherd to tell us something about God. Think about what a shepherd does and what a shepherd is like. How is God like a shepherd?

_____

_____

In the second verse, the poet describes "green pastures" and "still waters." Compare those images to the image of "the valley of the shadow of death." Those images have very different moods. In the table below, write down the moods or emotions that the images bring to you.

| _God makes me rest in green pastures_ _Leads me to still waters._ | _I walk through the valley of the shadow of death._ |
|---|---|
| Mood: | Mood: |

# Psalms of Holiness

One purpose of some of the psalms is to help us feel and understand the holiness of God. The feelings that a person has toward God are some of the most difficult feelings to describe. We can't see or touch God. Every person feels God in a unique way. How can we talk about something that we cannot touch or see? How can we share ideas when God means something different to each of us?

Below is a psalm that was written to help share those ideas of God's holiness:

*How lovely is Your dwelling place, Adonai Tz'vaot.*
*I long, I yearn for the courts of God;*
*My body and soul shout for joy to the living God.*
*Even the sparrow has a home,*
*And the swallow has her nest*
*In which to place her young*
*Near Your altar, Adonai Tz'vaot,*
*My ruler and my God.*
*Happy are those who live in Your House;*
*They praise You forever.*

PSALM 84:2–5

Choose an image or description from Psalm 84. Look for a word or idea in the text that grabs your attention or touches an emotion in you. Underline the verse or verses in which the image is found.

Next, copy the verse or verses in the space below.

_____

_____

_____

_____

_____

_____

_____

As you were reading or writing those words, what did the description remind you of? What other image or event in your life did you recall?

_____

_____

_____

What is the mood of the passage? How did reading it make you feel?

_____

_____

Below are lines from a poem by a famous modern rabbi, Rav Abraham Isaac Kook, who lived from 1865 to 1935. Rav Kook was a master at describing holiness. As you read his words, think about how alike and how different his images are from those in the psalm we just read.

*Expanses, expanses,*
*My soul craves divine expanses.*
*Do not lock me in cages,*
*Real or of spirit.*
*My soul soars the expanses of the*
  *heavens.*
*I am thirsty, I thirst for God,*
*Like a deer for a brook of water.*
*I see the flames rise up,*

*Piercing the sky,*
*But who feels, who can express their*
  *might?*
*My pain and suffering is great,*
*My God, my God, help me in my trouble,*
*Make it easy for me to express myself,*
*Give me the words and the gift to speak,*
*I shall tell everyone*
*My own piece of Your Truth, my God.*

RAV ABRAHAM ISAAC KOOK

Did Rav Kook use any images that are similar to those in the psalm? Which image or images are most alike?

_____

_____

Both poems describe what it is like wanting to be closer to God. Is that a hard idea to describe? Why or why not?

_____

_____

_____

# By the Rivers of Babylon

In chapter 15, we read about the Babylonian exile. By now you are familiar with what happened, how the Temple was destroyed and many of the people of Judah were taken into captivity in Babylon.

In that chapter we looked at some verses of Psalm 137. Let's take another look at it now and examine the images and emotions that were expressed during the exile:

*1 By the rivers of Babylon,*
*There we sat,*
*Sat and wept,*
*As we thought of Zion.*
*There on the poplars*
*We hung our lyres,*
*For our captors asked us for songs,*
*Our tormentors, to entertain them.*
*"Sing us one of your songs of Zion."*
*How can we sing a song of God in a*
*    strange land?*
*If I forget you Jerusalem,*

*May my right hand wither,*
*May my tongue stick in my mouth*
*If I stop thinking of you,*
*If I fail to keep Jerusalem in mind*
*Even at my happiest moments.*

PSALM 137:1–6

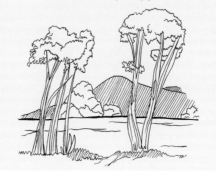

The person who wrote this psalm was probably living in Babylonia during the exile. This poet must have had a reason for writing it. What do you think is the purpose of the psalm?

_____

_____

_____

Look closely at the following passage from Psalm 137. In the space provided, describe the image and how it makes you feel, and point out any parallelisms in the verses.

| | |
|---|---|
| *If I forget you Jerusalem,*<br>*May my right hand wither,*<br>*May my tongue stick in my mouth* | _____<br>_____<br>_____<br>_____<br>_____<br>_____<br>_____<br>_____ |

# Proverbs

The second book of the *K'tuvim* section of the *Tanakh* is also a book of poetry. Just as legend says that King David wrote many of the psalms, King Solomon, it is said, wrote the Book of **Proverbs.** In reality, both books were written by several different authors. **Proverbs** may have been written about five hundred years after the time of King Solomon.

The book of **Proverbs** is a guidebook of practical wisdom. The purpose of the book is to teach the reader to be happy and successful in life. Each poem is a lesson about gaining wisdom and understanding and about being a good person.

The Hebrew name for this book is *Mishlei* מִשְׁלֵי, which comes from the word *mashal. Mashal* מָשָׁל is a comparison, analogy, or example.

**Proverbs** is all about wisdom. The poets who wrote **Proverbs** used many images as examples of what wisdom is like. Wisdom, they wrote, is a light. Wisdom is better than a fine jewel. Wisdom is a tree. Later, the Rabbis reinterpreted "teaching" and wisdom in the Book of **Proverbs** to mean the Torah.

Below is the opening of the Book of **Proverbs:**

These are the proverbs of Solomon son of David, king of Israel:

For learning wisdom and discipline,
For understanding words of deep meaning,
For keeping a positive and successful attitude,
Righteousness, justice, and fairness.

Respect for God is the beginning of knowledge.
Foolish ones hate wisdom and discipline.

Child, listen to the training of your father,
Do not ignore the teaching of your mother.
They are a crown on your head,
A necklace about your throat.

PROVERBS 1:1–3, 7–9

What, according to the text, is the beginning of knowledge?

_____

Explain what that means. How can that lead a person to knowledge?

_____

_____

_____

How is learning like a crown?

_____

_____

The next text is a short section from the third chapter of **Proverbs.** You may recognize it from the synagogue Torah service:

*Happy is the one who finds wisdom,*
*The one who gains understanding.*
*Her value is better than silver,*
*Her profits, more than gold.*
*She is more precious than rubies;*
*Nothing else can match her.*
*In her right hand is length of days,*
*In her left, riches and honor.*
*Her ways are ways of pleasantness,*
*And all her paths are peace.*

*She is a tree of life to those who*
*hold her,*
*Those who hang on to her are*
*happy.*

PROVERBS 3:13–18

How is Torah or learning like a tree? Below are the beginnings of several *m'shalim*, or analogies, about trees. Finish each sentence by adding in something—an object or an idea—related to Torah or learning.

The branches of a tree are like: _____.

The roots of a tree are like: _____.

The leaves of a tree are like: _____.

The shade of a tree is like: _____.

The fruits of a tree are like: _____.

The trunk of a tree is like: _____.

The age of a tree is like: _____.

Can you think of any other analogies about trees and Torah?

_____

_____

_____

_____

Here is a midrash from the *Taanit* volume of the Babylonian Talmud:

Rabbi Nachman bar Isaac asked: "Do you know why the words of Torah are compared to a tree, as in the verse 'She is a tree of life to those who hold her' (Proverbs 3:18)? It is to teach you that just as a small burning tree may set a big tree on fire, so can students sharpen the minds of greater scholars." Rabbi Chanina agreed with this, saying: "I have learned much from my teachers. I've learned even more from my friends. But from my students I have learned more than from anyone else."

BABYLONIAN TALMUD, *TAANIT* 7A

Explain the meaning of this midrash. What are the two rabbis telling us about learning?

_____

_____

The following is another section of **Proverbs**, taken from the sixth chapter. It also provides a lesson about Torah using *m'shalim*, or comparisons. You will also notice that it is a good example of parallelism. Each couplet of lines is an almost perfect parallel.

Child, keep your father's commands
   [mitzvot],
Do not forget your mother's teaching
   [Torah].
Tie them over your heart forever,
Attach it to your throat.
When you walk it will lead you.
When you rest it will protect you.
And when you are awake it will speak to
   you.
For the command [mitzvah] is a lamp,
And teaching [Torah] is light.

PROVERBS 6:20–23

Although the *p'shat* (plain sense) of these lines is that we should learn from our parents and obey them, the early Rabbis understood these lines to mean that our parents should teach us Torah and mitzvot, and that we should tie them to our hearts and attach them to our throats. Is this meant literally? Are we supposed to actually wear them like jewelry? Or is the text meant as a *mashal*, a symbol to compare it with something else? How can we wear Torah and mitzvot on our hearts and our throats?

_____

_____

_____

The text also says that Torah and mitzvot are a light and a lamp. What kind? What do you think this means? Is light a symbol, or *mashal*, for something else?

_____

_____

The Book of **Proverbs** contains wonderful words and images about the very thing you are doing now! It is about learning and thereby becoming a more successful, happy, and moral person. How can the study of *Tanakh* help you to be a happier, more successful, and good, moral person?

_____

_____

_____

*In this chapter, we read many examples of Hebrew poetry from the Books of **Psalms** and **Proverbs**. The purpose of these poems is to teach us about God and holiness, wisdom and learning. In the next chapter, we will continue learning about the K'tuvim—or Writings—section of the Bible by reading samples from the five m'gillot.*

# Chapter Twenty-One

## THE FIVE *M'GILLOT*

*The **Psalms**, more than any other collection of poetry, have made a lasting impression on our prayer service. We can hardly sing a medley of Jewish songs without having the words of **Psalms** come from our lips. But what of other books in the Bible? Five times a year, on five specific Holy Days, we read one of the five m'gillot, or scrolls. In this chapter, we will learn about those scrolls, where they come from, and when we read them.*

# The Five Scrolls

Other than the Torah and the Book of **Psalms** *(T'hilim),* nothing in the Bible has as important a role in modern Jewish holiday observance as the five *m'gillot.* The word *m'gillah* means "scroll" and comes from a Hebrew root meaning "to turn." (The root *galal* is also found in the Hebrew word for wheel, *galgal.)*

You may recognize the word "megillah" from a popular English slang expression, "the whole megillah." When someone is talking about **all** of something, or the whole story, or when they are saying that something is very involved or complicated, sometimes they call it "the whole megillah."

The most familiar of the *m'gillot* is *M'gillat Ester,* the Book of **Esther,** which we read each year on Purim. There are four other scrolls that we use for holiday observance. Each of the five scrolls is included in the *K'tuvim* section of the *Tanakh.*

The five *m'gillot* are:

> **Song of Songs** *(Shir HaShirim),* which we read on Passover
>
> **Ruth** *(Rut),* which we read on Shavuot
>
> **Lamentations** *(Eichah),* which we read on Tishah B'Av
>
> **Ecclesiastes** *(Kohelet),* which we read on Sukkot
>
> **Esther** *(Ester),* which we read on Purim

# Song of Songs

The first of the *m'gillot* is a collection of love poems. Love poems? If you are wondering what love poems are doing in the Bible, you are not alone. Rabbis and scholars have been wondering the same thing for two thousand years. The word for the official table of contents of the Bible, what goes in and what doesn't, is "canon." It's possible that there were arguments over whether or not to include **Song of Songs** in the Bible. We don't know exactly how **Song of Songs** came to be included in the biblical canon, but it did!

In early Israelite times, there were probably many collections of love poetry. Historians think that these were read or sung as part of the wedding ceremony. Of all these collections, only one survives: **Song of Songs,** or *Shir HaShirim* שִׁיר הַשִּׁירִים in Hebrew.

The collection begins:

> The Song of Songs of Solomon:
> *Let him give me the kisses of your mouth,*
> *For your love is sweeter than wine.*
>
> SONG OF SONGS 1:1–2

No one knows for certain if King Solomon had anything at all to do with this collection of poems. It is not likely that he actually wrote any of it. One reason why this book was included in the canon is that some people thought it was written by Israel's king.

Why do you think King Solomon's name appears at the beginning of **Song of Songs?**

____ Because "Solomon" like "Song" begins with the letter "S" (שׁ in Hebrew).

____ Because in I Kings 11:1 we are told "King Solomon loved many foreign women."

____ Because it was written by someone else named Solomon.

**Song of Songs** uses beautiful and natural images to describe human love. As people read these poems, they will be reminded of spring and nature and love. Within these poems, some verses appear to be written by a man, and others appear to be written by a woman. Below is a passage that seems to be told by a woman describing the man that she loves:

*Listen, I hear my love,*
*Here he comes,*
*Leaping over mountains,*
*Bounding over hills.*
*My lover is like a gazelle,*
*Like a young stag,*
*He is standing behind our wall,*
*Looking through the window,*
*Peering through the shades.*

*My lover said to me:*
*"Arise, my darling,*
*My fair one, come away!*
*For now the winter has passed,*
*The rains are over and gone.*
*The blossoms have appeared on the land,*
*The time of singing has come.*
*The song of the turtledove*
*Is heard in the land.*

> *The green figs grow on the fig tree,*
> *The blossoming vines smell sweet.*
> *Arise, my darling,*
> *My fair one, come away."*

> . . . . . . . . . . . . . . . . . . . . . . . . . . . . . . . . . . . . . . . .
> *My lover is mine,*
> *And I am his.*
>
> SONG OF SONGS 2:8–13, 16

Over the years, rabbis have explained **Song of Songs** as a metaphor for the love between God and Israel. Others have said that it is a statement that nature (including love and sex) is an important part of God's creation. In the space provided, explain both opinions.

| **Song of Songs** describes the love between God and the people Israel. | **Song of Songs** teaches us that nature and love are part of God's creation. |
| --- | --- |
| _____ | _____ |
| _____ | _____ |
| _____ | _____ |
| _____ | _____ |
| _____ | _____ |

# Ruth

The second of the *m'gillot* is the Book of **Ruth,** which is read during the Festival of Shavuot, when we remember the grain harvest and the giving of the Torah at Sinai. **Ruth** is the story of a non-Israelite woman who joined the Israelite people and became the great-grandmother of King David.

In the days when the judges ruled, there was a famine in the land. A man named Elimelech from Bethlehem in Judah took his wife and two sons and moved to Moab. His wife was named Naomi, and his sons were named Mahlon and Chilion.

Elimelech died, and Naomi was left alone with her two sons. Eventually, the two sons married Moabite women, one named Orpah, the other named Ruth.

After about ten years, the two sons, Mahlon and Chilion, died.

Left alone with no husband and no sons, Naomi decided to return home from Moab, since she had heard that God had brought an end to the famine. Naomi told her two daughters-in-law, "You should each go back to your mother's house. May God be as kind to you as you have been to the dead and to me. May God see that each of you finds a new husband."

She kissed them goodbye, and they broke out crying. "No, we will go back with you to your people."

Naomi said, "Go back, my daughters. There is no reason for you to come with me. I have no more sons for you to marry. I can't provide for you."

They began crying again. Orpah kissed her mother-in-law goodbye. But Ruth stayed with her.

Naomi said, "Please do as your sister-in-law has done. Go back to your own people and your own gods."

Ruth said, "Don't make me leave you. Wherever you go, I shall go. Wherever you live, I shall live. Your people shall be my people, and your God shall be my God...."

And so Naomi returned from the land of Moab with her daughter-in-law Ruth the Moabite. They arrived in Bethlehem at the beginning of the barley harvest.

Now, Naomi had a relative named Boaz, who was a wealthy man. Ruth the Moabite said to Naomi, "I would like to go to the fields and gather ears of grain, by someone who will show me kindness."

"Yes, daughter. Go."

She went off and came to a piece of land belonging to Boaz. She began gleaning behind the reapers. Soon, Boaz arrived from Bethlehem and said, "God bless you," to the reapers. They said, "God bless you," to him. Then Boaz asked the foreman in charge of the reapers, "Who is that woman?"

He replied, "She is the Moabite woman who came back with Naomi. She asked if she could gather the fallen grain behind the reapers. She has been working hard all day."

RUTH 1:1–16, 22; 2:1–7

# Lamentations

The third of the *m'gillot* is read on Tishah B'Av—the Ninth of Av—when we commemorate the destruction of the First and Second Temples in Jerusalem. **Lamentations** (*Eichah* אֵיכָה in Hebrew) is a set of five poems about the destruction of the First Temple. Tradition tells us that the prophet Jeremiah wrote this book. In truth, we don't know who the author of **Lamentations** was, but it was probably composed during the Babylonian exile.

As you read the following passage, notice how Jerusalem is described in almost human terms:

*Lonely sits the city*
*Once filled with people.*
*She who was great among the nations*
*Is now like a widow.*

· · · · · · · · · · · · · · · · · · · · · · · · · · · · · · · · · · · · · · · ·

*All her valuables*
*From the days of old*
*Jerusalem remembered*
*In her days of sadness and sorrow.*
*When her people fell by enemy hands*
*With none to help her.*

*When enemies looked on and laughed*
*Over her downfall.*

*Jerusalem has sinned terribly.*
*So she has become a mockery,*
*All who admired her now hate her,*
*They have seen her disgraced,*
*And she can only sigh*
*And shrink back.*

LAMENTATIONS 1:1, 7–8

Throughout much of **Lamentations**, Jerusalem is described as a woman. Choose from the above passage one of the lines that depicts Jerusalem as a woman, and write it below.

_____

_____

What is the purpose of that image? What does it tell us about how the author saw Jerusalem?

_____

_____

# Ecclesiastes

During the autumn festival of Sukkot, Jewish traditon teaches that we should read the Book of **Ecclesiastes,** or *Kohelet* קֹהֶלֶת. The name *Kohelet* means "Assembler," "Teacher," or "Preacher." It comes from the same root as the word *k'hilah,* which means "community," "congregation," or "synagogue." Most English-language Bibles call this book "Ecclesiastes" ("Convoker" or "Preacher"), from the Greek name of the book.

In the opening line of **Ecclesiastes,** the author announces that he is the son of David, king of Jerusalem. That has led people to think that King Solomon wrote it. Many of the lines within the book also point to Solomon. But, as with **Proverbs** and **Song of Songs,** it is very unlikely that Solomon had anything to do with writing this book.

> The words of Kohelet, son of David, king of Jerusalem.
>
> Vanity of vanities, said Kohelet
> Vanity of vanities, all is vanity.
>
> *What is the real meaning for a person*
> *Of all the pursuits under the sun?*
>
> ECCLESIASTES 1:1–3

Vanity means emptiness. Just as a weather vane turns according to the wind, so do our lives at times seem to amount to nothing but air and emptiness. Every autumn, as we watch the leaves turn and fall, as we watch all of nature seem to die until spring, it is very easy for people to take stock in their lives. We might ask ourselves, if we all die anyway, what is the point of living?

During Sukkot, as we sit in our booths surrounded by fruit, it is easy to remember the serious questions we asked ourselves during Rosh HaShanah and Yom Kippur. Why am I here? What do I matter? These are the questions that the author of **Ecclesiastes** asks us.

The speaker in **Ecclesiastes** tells us that he tried many different lifestyles to try to find happiness.

First he tried wisdom. He read every book he could find, but soon found that it didn't make him any happier.

Then he tried pleasure—eating, drinking, and playing as hard as he could to have fun. But fun didn't make him any happier.

Next he tried riches, working hard to amass more gold and property than anyone else. But money didn't make him happy.

The answer to life's meaning is a hard one to grasp. But the Book of **Ecclesiastes** does give us a surprising answer. In the next chapter, we will explore that answer, along with the lessons of the Book of **Job.**

Like Kohelet, we all want to be happy. What do you do to try to find happiness?

_____

_____

_____

# Esther

The Book of **Esther** tells of a Persian king, Ahasuerus, who became angry with his wife, Vashti, and decided to choose a new wife.

In the fortress city of Shushan lived a Jew by the name of Mordecai son of Jair, a Benjaminite. His great-grandfather was among those who was exiled from Jerusalem by King Nebuchadnezzar of Babylon. He was the foster father of Esther, his uncle's daughter, who was an orphan. She was shapely and beautiful, and when her parents died, Mordecai adopted her as his own daughter.

When the king's order was proclaimed and many young women were brought together in Shushan, Esther was brought in under the supervision of Hegai, the guardian of women....

Esther was taken to King Ahasuerus in his royal palace in the tenth month, that is Tevet, in the seventh year of his reign. The king loved Esther more than all the other women, and she won his grace and favor. So he set a crown on her head and made her queen instead of Vashti. The king gave a great banquet for all his officials and friends. He proclaimed a tax amnesty and provided gifts. Esther, meanwhile, had not revealed her ancestry or nationality.

Around this time, Mordecai was sitting in the palace gate. Two of the king's servants, Bigthan and Teresh, were angry with the king and were plotting to assassinate him.

When Mordecai heard, he told Queen Esther, who in turn told the king in Mordecai's name. The case was looked into, and the two men were found guilty and sentenced to death. The case was recorded in the king's record book.

Some time later, King Ahasuerus promoted Haman son of Hammedatha the Agagite. He gave him a position higher than any other official. Everyone bowed low to Haman at the palace gate, as the king ordered. But Mordecai would not kneel or bow.

ESTHER 2:5–8, 16–23; 3:1–2

As the story continues, Haman decided to get his revenge on Mordecai's stubbornness by ordering that on the thirteenth day of Adar, all Jews in Persia would be killed. In the end, due to Mordecai's wisdom and Esther's courage, Haman's plan was reversed. Haman and all his family were hung on the very same gallows that had been set up for the Jews. The Jews of Persia were saved, and Mordecai was recognized as a hero.

Mordecai left the king dressed in royal robes of blue and white, with a magnificent crown of gold and a coat of fine linen and purple wool. The city of Shushan rang with joyous cries. The Jews celebrated with happiness and honor. In every province and in every city, when the king's command was announced, there was gladness and joy among the Jews. They had a feast and a holiday. Many people now pretended to be Jews, because they now feared them.

ESTHER 8:15–17

What is the purpose of the Book of **Esther**? In telling a story of the courage of Esther and Mordecai, and of the defeat of Haman, how did the author want his audience to feel?

_____

_____

_____

*In this chapter, we have looked at five books from the Writings—K'tuvim—section of the* Tanakh. *These five books—**Song of Songs**, **Ruth**, **Lamentations**, **Ecclesiastes**, and **Esther**—are the five* m'gillot *read on the Holy Days of Passover, Shavuot, Tishah B'Av, Sukkot, and Purim. In our next chapter, we will take a closer and deeper look at **Ecclesiastes**, along with the Book of **Job**.*

# Chapter Twenty-Two

# WISDOM BOOKS: JOB AND ECCLESIASTES

*What is the meaning of life? Why do good people suffer? These are two of the most important and most difficult questions that religion tries to answer. In this chapter, we will look at two biblical books that attempt to answer them.*

People often say that religion gives us comfort and easy answers to life's problems. However, there are two books in the Bible that ask very hard questions and provide neither comfort nor easy answers:

- Why do people suffer?
- What can I do to be happy?

When people first read **Job** and **Ecclesiastes,** they are often struck by the fact that the books don't seem to answer these questions at all. **Job** seems to say that there is no reason why people suffer. **Ecclesiastes** seems to say that there is nothing that can make us happy because everything is meaningless.

These two books **do** provide answers. But the answers are hard to see at first. The answers are some of the Bible's most beautiful writing. And these answers have been interpreted differently by different people over the ages. But one lesson is certain: life's hard questions do not have easy answers.

In the early 1970s, Rabbi Harold Kushner was faced with one of these lessons. His son Aaron, while still a child, was losing his hair and physically deteriorating the way people normally do when they get old. The doctors diagnosed Aaron with a disease called progeria, which caused his body to age much faster than was normal. At the age most kids were playing baseball and practicing for bar mitzvah, Aaron was dying of old age. Rabbi Kushner was angry, sad, and upset all at the same time. Aaron was a good boy from a good family. Rabbi Kushner had devoted his life to serving God and the Jewish people. How could this happen to him?

Shortly after Aaron Kushner died in 1977, Rabbi Kushner began writing a book that explored the problem of why bad things happen. He came to the conclusion—after reexamining the Book of **Job**—that there is no satisfying reason **why** bad things happen to good people. Sometimes bad things just happen. The question should be: what do we do when bad things happen? Rabbi Kushner's book, *When Bad Things Happen to Good People,* was published in 1981 and has helped thousands of people cope with tragedy.

Just as Rabbi Kushner did, we will now turn to the Book of **Job** to begin asking the question of why people suffer.

# Job: Why Do People Suffer?

Judaism teaches many things about God. Among these teachings, three themes always come up. These are three assumptions that we have about God:

- God is omniscient: God sees and knows everything;
- God is omnipotent: God can do anything;
- God is moral: God is good. God cares about people and doesn't want them to suffer.

All the earlier books of the Bible have suggested that God **rewards** good behavior and **punishes** bad behavior. Every time the people of Israel lost a battle or suffered exile, the prophets told the people it was because they had done something bad in God's eyes.

The author of **Job** uses his story to tell us that justice is not quite so simple. Bad things do happen to good people. When a child is killed by disease or by auto accident, it is not because the child is being punished for doing something wrong. Innocent children do die. Good people suffer cancer and storms and car wrecks. The character of Job is one of these people, and he wanted to know why.

As the story opens, God and some of the angels were discussing what a good man Job is:

There was a man in the land of Uz named Job. He was faultless and honest. He had respected God and avoided evil. He had seven sons and three daughters. His property included seven thousand sheep, three thousand camels, five hundred head of ox, and five hundred donkeys. He had a huge estate. He was the richest man in the East....

One day, the celestial beings, including the Satan, met before God. God asked Satan, "Where have you been?"

Satan said, "I've been wandering around the earth."

God said, "Did you happen to see My servant Job? There is no one like him on earth. He is a faultless and honest man who respects God and avoids evil."

The Satan said, "Job has good reason to respect God. You have protected him and his household. You have blessed everything he does so that his property spreads out over the whole country. But if You ever hurt him, he would be certain to curse You to Your face."

God said, "All right, do whatever you like with him, but you may not physically harm him."

Satan left from God's presence.

JOB 1:1–3, 6–12

217

# The Heavenly Court

Jewish readers are sometimes surprised when they read the opening of **Job**. If there is only one God in heaven and earth, then who are all these beings with God? And what is Satan doing in a Jewish story?

The truth is that Jewish legend and folklore is full of heavenly beings. In previous chapters, we have already encountered angels, cherubim, and seraphim. These may have originally been used to symbolize ideas or parts of God. They may be leftover traditions from the days before monotheism. They may just be stories. Or they may be real. We don't know.

Jews do not believe in a Satan who was an angel who fell from grace and now rules hell with pitchfork. Jews do not believe in a Satan who is God's opposite and who will fight God for the souls at the end of time. These are not the Satan that we find in the Book of **Job**. The Hebrew word *satan* שָׂטָן means one who is opposite or opposed, an adversary. The character of Satan in Job seems to be an angelic being who serves a lawyer-like job of prosecuting attorney.

# The Story

As soon as God sent Satan on his way, bad things began happening to Job.

First, his oxen and donkeys were stolen.

Then a fire came out of the sky and killed all his sheep and shepherds.

Then his camels were stolen by Chaldeans (Babylonians), who then killed his farmhands.

And finally, a huge gust of wind destroyed the home of one of Job's sons, while the rest of Job's sons and daughters were visiting. Everyone in the house was killed.

How do you think Job reacted to all these disasters? He went into mourning.

Job got up, tore his robe, cut off his hair, and threw himself down on the ground and prayed. "I came out of my mother's womb naked, and naked I shall return. God gives and God takes away. Blessed be the name of God."

JOB 1:20–21

Job demonstrated some of the standard mourning rituals of the time. It was common, upon hearing tragic news, to tear one's garment, to put ashes on one's head, and to wear a rough, uncomfortable garment made of sackcloth.

It is still common today that when Jews hear tragic news about the death of a family member, they tear their shirt and say:

BARUCH DAYAN HA-EMET.

בָּרוּךְ דַּיָן הָאֱמֶת

"BLESSED BE THE TRUE JUDGE."

But this doesn't account for why Job did what he did. He was a man who had everything, and suddenly he lost everything, including his children. What did Job mean by his statement "I came out of my mother's womb naked, and naked I shall return. God gives and God takes away. Blessed be the name of God"?

_____

_____

_____

Was Job's response appropriate to the tragedies? If so, why? If not, what should he have done?

_____

_____

_____

When Satan returned to God's presence, God was pleased to point out that Job had remained upright and God-fearing. Satan responded, "Of course. But if you let me hurt him physically I will be able to prove my point." Satan then gave Job sores all over his body so that he was swollen and itching all over.

Seeing her husband look so pathetic, Job's wife became angry and said:

"Why are you still being so upright? Curse God and die!" Job answered her: "You speak without shame. Should we accept only good from God and not accept evil?" And still, Job said nothing sinful.　　　　JOB 2:9–10

Why do you think Job's wife told her husband to "curse God and die"? What did she mean by that?

_____

_____

Explain Job's response, "Should we accept only good from God and not accept evil?" What did he mean?

_____

_____

The American poet Archibald MacLeish wrote a play based on the Book of **Job**. It was titled *J.B.* and was a success on Broadway in 1957.

Here's how MacLeish wrote the discussion between Job and his wife:

J.B. *(a whisper):* God, let me die!
Sarah *(her voice dead):* You think He'd help you even to that? God is our enemy.
J.B.: No ... No ... No ... Don't say that Sarah! God has something hidden from our hearts to show. Try to sleep.

Sarah *(bitterly):* He should have kept it hidden.
J.B.: Sleep now.
Sarah: You don't have to see it: I do.
J.B.: Yes, I know.

In what ways is the MacLeish version of the story different from the Bible's?

_____

_____

In what ways are they similar?

_____

_____

Do you think MacLeish did a good job capturing the feelings of the two characters?
Write your own dialogue between Job and his wife.

Job: _____

_____

Mrs. Job: _____

_____

Job: _____

_____

Mrs. Job: _____

_____

Job: _____

_____

Mrs. Job: _____

_____

Job: _____

_____

Mrs. Job _____

_____

Job: _____

_____

# Job's Friends

After Job's wife made her comment, three of Job's friends arrived to console their friend. The names of the men are Eliphaz of Teman, Bildad of Shuah, and Zophar of Naamat. They came and sat and remained quiet for seven days.

This event gives us a window into some mourning practices that were followed at the time the Book of **Job** was written—practices that are still followed today. It is customary in Jewish families that when a member dies, the immediate family remains in the house for seven days. This tradition is called "sitting shivah" from the Hebrew word for the number seven *(shivah* שִׁבְעָה*)*.

While a family is sitting shivah, it is customary for friends, neighbors, and relatives to come over and visit, bringing gifts of food.

What are you supposed to say to someone you know who has just lost a husband, wife, parent, or other close relative? People find this to be one of the most awkward situations to be in. Yet it is considered one of the highest mitzvot to visit a "house of mourning" and to comfort the mourners. And what is the best thing to say? The less, the better. As in the case of Job and his friends, it is usually best to let the mourner speak first. But unlike Job's friends, it is best to say warm and supportive things.

Have you ever visited a family that was sitting shivah? Have you attended a funeral or memorial service? Use the space below to write down your feelings. What thoughts went through your head? Was it awkward? Embarrassing? Sad?

When Job's seven days of mourning ended, he began to speak. He was bitter. He complained. But he never criticized God. Rather, he said:

Perish the day that I was born,
The night it was announced:
"It's a boy!"
May that day be darkness;
May God ignore it;

May light not shine on it.
...............................................................
Why couldn't I have died at birth,
Stillborn as I came out from the womb?

JOB 3:3–4, 11

After Job finished speaking, his friends, each in turn, spoke to Job. Their comments to him contained beautiful words, but they were of no comfort to him. Each in his own way told Job: You must have done something wrong. You might not remember it. It might have been something very small. But you did something wrong, or else God wouldn't do this to you.

After each of his friends' speeches, Job responded with a speech of his own, each time saying that he was blameless.

A fourth friend, a man named Elihu, joined the debate by saying in stronger terms: It is wrong to say that you are blameless. God is greater than any human.

# God's Response

In the midst of Elihu's speech, a whirlwind broke out, and the voice of God called down on them:

Who is this who darkens the debate,
Speaking without knowing?
Brace yourself, be strong,
I will ask and you will answer.

Where were you when I laid the earth's
  foundation?
Speak if you know the answer.
Do you know who fixed its dimensions

Or measured its lines?
Where were the bases sunk?
Who set the cornerstone
When the morning stars sang together
And the angels shouted for joy?

Who closed the sea behind the floodgates
When it gushed out of the womb,
When I clothed it in clouds,

When I made the shores to stop it,
And set up its bar and doors,
And said, "Come no further,
This is where your waves will break"?

Have you ever called on morning to come,
Assigned the dawn its place,
So that it grabs the edge of the earth
And shakes the wicked up?

. . . . . . . . . . . . . . . . . . . . . . . . . . . . . .

Does rain have a father?
Who mothered the dewdrops?
From whose belly did the ice form?
Who gave birth to the frosty skies?
Water hardens like stone,
And the surface of the ocean grows hard.

Can you tie ropes to Pleiades
Or undo Orion's belt?
Can you guide the Morning Star by its
    season?
Show the Bear to her cubs?

Can you send up an order to the clouds,
For more water to cover you?
Can you send lightning for a trip,
And have it tell you, "At your service"?

. . . . . . . . . . . . . . . . . . . . . . . . . . . . . .

Do you give the horse its strength?
Do you clothe its neck with a mane?
Do you make him leap like a cricket,
His proud neighing snorting bravely?

. . . . . . . . . . . . . . . . . . . . . . . . . . . . . .

Is it by your wisdom that the hawk flies,
Spreading its wings to the south?
Does the eagle soar at your command,
Building its nest high?
She sleeps in the rocky crags,
Lodging in a mountain peak.

JOB 38:1–13, 28–32, 34–35,
39:19–20, 26–28

God described one after another part of nature, part of God's creation. The descriptions are beautiful and frightening at the same time.

In the end, after God had spoken, Job replied:

I know that You are all-powerful
You can do whatever You plan.
I am the one who confuses Your plans
With my empty-headed words.
I have been debating over things I cannot
    understand,
On subjects beyond my scope and
    knowledge.

Listen while I speak,
I ask and You will answer me.
I have heard of You with my ears
But now I see You with my eyes.
I take back what I said.
I am but dust and ashes.

JOB 42:1–6

God answered Job with images from nature, from God's creation. Which of God's descriptions did you most enjoy?

_____

_____

Describe how it made you feel.

_____

_____

Why do you think God responded with images from nature?

_____

_____

How did God's response answer Job's problems?

_____

_____

In Job's response to God, he said,

> I have heard of You with my ears
> But now I see You with my eyes.

What was it that Job saw?

_____

_____

# Ecclesiastes: What Can I Do to Be Happy?

In chapter 21, we briefly looked at the Book of **Ecclesiastes**—or *Kohelet*—one of the five *m'gillot*. **Ecclesiastes** is one of the most wondrous books of the *Tanakh*. It is also one of the most baffling.

The author of **Ecclesiastes** asks two very difficult questions:

- If everyone dies, what difference does it make if I'm good or bad?
- When I have everything I ever wanted, why am I still unhappy?

There are many memorable themes that run through **Ecclesiastes.** You may have heard them in other contexts. They were first used in **Ecclesiastes.** Here are a few of them:

- "Vanity of vanities": For the author of **Ecclesiastes,** "vanity" (hevel הֶבֶל) meant something that was filled with air or wind. (We use the term today when we refer to a weather vane.) To Kohelet, everything was empty—full of wind.
- "Nothing new under the sun": For Kohelet, nothing seemed to change. No one could claim to have done something special because everything had been done before. Nothing was new.
- "Chasing after wind": Imagine someone trying to chase his or her shadow, or a horse running after a carrot on a stick. As fast and as hard as they run, they will never reach their goal. **Ecclesiastes** uses this image to show that whatever a person wants to get, they can never have enough, always wanting more.

The opening line of **Ecclesiastes** suggests that the author was King Solomon. As we learned earlier in this book, that is unlikely. **Ecclesiastes** contains style and ideas from a much later period. The name *Kohelet* means "Assembler" or "Teacher" and is often translated as "Preacher." Here is the opening of the book of **Ecclesiastes:**

*The words of Kohelet, son of David, king of Jerusalem.*

*Vanity of vanities, said Kohelet,
Vanity of vanities, All is vanity.
What real value is there for a person of all the pursuits under the sun?
A generation goes and another one comes.
But the earth remains the same forever.
The sun rises and the sun sets.
It always goes back to where it started.*

. . . . . . . . . . . . . . . . . . . . . . . . . . . . . . . . . . . . . . . .

*Whatever was will be again,*

*There's nothing new under the sun.*

*Anytime something comes up,*

*And people say, "This is unique,"*

*It's been before, long ago.*

*We don't remember earlier times,*

*Just as today will be forgotten.*

I am Kohelet, king in Jerusalem over Israel. I set my mind to study and to probe all wisdom that exists under the sun. Now that is the most depressing job that God has given us! I studied all things under the sun, and I found that it was futile, like chasing after the wind.

*What is twisted cannot be straightened.*

*What isn't there cannot be counted.*

I told myself, "I am wiser than anyone who ruled before me over Jerusalem. My mind is so absorbed with wisdom and learning." I was dedicated to wisdom; and also to stupidity and folly. I now know that it is chasing after wind.

*Much wisdom, much sadness,*

*More knowledge, more sorrow.*

So I said to myself, "It's time for pleasure. Let's have some fun." But that too is vanity.

*Laughter is madness,*

*Pleasure is pointless.*

I cheered myself up with wine in order to learn pleasure. I decided to make a study to see which is a better pursuit for human beings to follow in their short lives under heaven, wisdom or pleasure. I acquired many things.

I built houses and I planted vineyards. I made gardens and groves and planted every kind of fruit tree. I built pools big enough to water a rainforest. I bought slaves, male and female, and hired servants. I had more cattle, herds, and flocks than anyone ever had in Jerusalem. I gathered silver and gold and treasures of kings. I hired entertainers and had all sorts of luxuries.

I had more wealth than anyone before me in Jerusalem. And I still kept my wisdom. Anytime my eyes wanted something, I took it. I didn't deny myself any pleasure. My wealth gave me much pleasure. But that is all it gave me.

Then I looked at all the fortune and wealth I had built up and oh! It was vanity and chasing after wind. There is nothing to be gained under the sun.

ECCLESIASTES 1:1–5, 9–18; 2:1–11

The narrator was discouraged by the fact that everyone dies. The wise person and the fool, the saint and the criminal will all end up dead in the ground. So what, he asked, is the point of being one over the other? What difference does it make?

In truth, Jews believe that people do make a difference. We make a difference through the good actions we perform. We make a difference by following the path of godliness. In the Ten Commandments, God tells us:

> I will visit the guilt of the parents upon the children, upon the third and fourth generations of those who reject Me, but showing kindness to the thousandth generation of those who love Me and keep My commandments.
>
> EXODUS 20:5–6

What are some of the ways that your actions can make a difference to the future? List three specific things that you can do that will have a lasting positive effect on the world.

1. _____

2. _____

3. _____

In the previous text, Kohelet said:

> Anytime my eyes wanted something, I took it. I didn't deny myself any pleasure. My wealth gave me much pleasure. But that is all it gave me. Then I looked at all the fortune and wealth I had built up and oh! It was vanity and chasing after wind.
>
> ECCLESIASTES 2:10–11

What did the author mean by the line: "I didn't deny myself any pleasure"?

_____

_____

_____

People still struggle to get more and more money, or wisdom, or games, or books. There is nothing wrong with any of these things. But Kohelet is telling us that they won't bring us happiness.

Think about something that you once wanted very badly and eventually got. How did it feel to have gotten it? Did it still matter a year later?

_____

_____

_____

In the midst of his discussion, Kohelet gives us this haunting poem, which tells that God has planned everything on God's own schedule:

A season is set for everything,
A time for every experience under heaven;
A time to be born, a time to die,
A time for planting, a time for pulling up,
A time to kill, a time to heal,
A time to destroy, a time to build,
A time to laugh, a time to cry,
A time to mourn, a time to dance,
A time to throw stones, a time to gather stones,
A time to hug, a time not to hug,
A time to seek, a time to lose,
A time to keep, a time to throw away,
A time to rip, a time to mend,
A time for silence, a time to talk,
A time for love, a time to hate,
A time for war, a time for peace.

ECCLESIASTES 3:1–8

What do you think is the author's purpose in writing the above passage? Try to rephrase and summarize the message of **Ecclesiastes** 3:1–8.

_____

_____

_____

_____

*Ecclesiastes* and *Job* are two of the many wisdom books of the Tanakh. Rather than giving us a lesson in history or in how to please God, these books challenge us to think. Rather than giving us comfort in easy, reassuring answers, these books force us to look at difficult questions and struggle to find answers on our own. In the next chapter, we will wrap up our study of the books of Prophets and Writings by looking at the last books of the Bible—**Daniel, Chronicles,** and *Ezra/Nehemiah.*

# Chapter Twenty-Three

# THE FINAL BOOKS: CHRONICLES, EZRA, NEHEMIAH, AND DANIEL

*As we conclude our study of* N'vi-im *and* K'tuvim, *the Prophets and Writings of the Bible, we come to several books that were among the last to be added to the Bible. These books give us a glimpse of the direction in which Judaism went as it passed from the biblical period to the age of the Rabbis and Talmud.*

The final books of the Hebrew Bible include stories and histories that wrap up the biblical period. The Books of **Samuel** and **Kings** told of the rise of a monarchy in Israel and then its split into two kingdoms. Isaiah prophesied in the years before the Assyrians destroyed the Northern Kingdom of Israel. Jeremiah wrote during a time when the Babylonians were gaining strength and Nebuchadnezzar prepared to conquer Judah. Ezekiel was among the prisoners taken into Babylonian captivity.

# Chronicles

Among the final Bible books to be written was a short history, retelling the entire story of the Jewish people from Adam—through Abraham, Moses, Joshua, and David—until the destruction of Jerusalem by King Nebuchadnezzar of Babylon. In Hebrew, this book is called *Divrei HaYamim* דִּבְרֵי הַיָּמִים—"The Matters of the Days"—and it is the final book in the *Tanakh*. (Most Christian Bibles place **Chronicles** right after **Samuel** and **Kings**.) The English name of this book is **Chronicles**, which means "Book of the Times." Like **Samuel** and **Kings**, **Chronicles** has been split into two books, **First Chronicles** (I Chronicles) and **Second Chronicles** (II Chronicles).

The following passage comes from the end of **Chronicles** and gives a summary of the last three kings of Judah, the destruction of Jerusalem, and the rise of a new Persian empire that would help the Jews return to their land and restore the Temple.

Jehoiakim was twenty-five years old when he became king. He ruled eleven years in Jerusalem. He did what was displeasing to *Adonai* his God. King Nebuchadnezzar of Babylon marched against him, put him in chains, and brought him to Babylon. Nebuchadnezzar also brought some of the vessels from the House of God to Babylon and set them in his palace....

Jehoiachin was eight years old when he became king, and he reigned three months and ten days in Jerusalem....

Zedekiah was twenty-one years old when he became king, and he reigned eleven years in Jerusalem. He did what was displeasing to *Adonai* his God. He refused to listen to God's prophet Jeremiah.... All the officers and priests and people committed many sins, doing as the other nations do. They defiled the Temple of God which God had consecrated in Jerusalem....

So God sent the king of the Chaldeans to attack them, to kill their soldiers at the Temple. They spared no one, including women and children, the old and the crippled. All the vessels and treasures of the Temple, large and small, were taken to Babylon along with the royal treasures. They burned the Temple of God and tore down the walls of Jerusalem, destroying homes and property. The survivors were exiled to Babylon, and they became servants of Nebuchadnezzar's son until the rise of the Persian empire....

And to fulfill the word that God had spoken by Jeremiah, in the first year of the reign of King Cyrus of Persia, God roused the spirit of King Cyrus who issued the following statement:

"These are the words of King Cyrus of Persia: *Adonai* God of Heaven has given me all the kingdoms of the earth. God has asked me to build Him a Temple in Jerusalem in the state of Judah. Any of you who are one of His people, may God be with him. Let him go up."

II CHRONICLES 36:5–7, 9, 11–12, 14, 17–20, 22–23

## King Cyrus of Persia

Not all Jewish heroes are Jewish. When Cyrus, the king of the Persian empire, conquered Babylon in 539 B.C.E., the Jewish people found themselves under friendly foreign government.

After taking control of Judah, King Cyrus of Persia invited all the exiled Jews to return to their homeland. He provided money and support to rebuild Jerusalem and the Temple. (After several stops and starts, the rebuilding of the Temple was completed about twenty years later.)

In the Book of **Isaiah** (in the sections written by "Second Isaiah"), Cyrus is called God's "shepherd" and "anointed one." It seems strange that a non-Jew would be considered so special to God in a book written by Jews. Why do you think Cyrus is called God's anointed and God's shepherd?

_____

_____

_____

# Ezra/Nehemiah

Continuing at the very point where the Book of **Chronicles** leaves off, the Books of **Ezra** and **Nehemiah** carry on the history of the rebuilding of Jerusalem. Originally these books were a single book. They tell similar stories and were probably written around the time that **Chronicles** was written.

The character of Ezra was neither a king nor a prophet nor a judge. He was a scribe. Nehemiah, on the other hand, was the royal cupbearer of the king of Persia. Although they both appear in these books and lived during roughly the same time, it isn't clear from the text whether the two men ever met.

King Cyrus of Persia issued his decree inviting the Jews to return to their land and rebuild their city. This was cause for a great celebration among the Jews.

> The chiefs of the clans of Judah and Benjamin, as well as the priests and Levites, everyone who had been inspired by God, got ready to go up and build the Temple of God in Jerusalem. Their neighbors helped them by giving silver and gold vessels, provisions, livestock, and precious objects. King Cyrus of Persia returned vessels of God's Temple that Nebuchadnezzar had taken away from Jerusalem.
>
> EZRA 1:5–7

Next, with the support of Cyrus, the Israelites began construction on a new Temple:

> When the builders had laid the foundation of the Temple of God, priests in their robes with trumpets and Levites with cymbals were stationed to give praise to God, just as King David had said. They sang songs praising God: "God is good. God's love for Israel is eternal." Everyone shouted out loud praising God because the foundation of the Temple had been laid. Many of the priests and family leaders and elders who had seen the first Temple wept loudly at the sight of the new Temple being built. Others shouted joyously as loud as they could. It was hard to tell the shouts of joy from the weeping, it was so loud. You could hear it from far off.
>
> EZRA 3:10–13

Not everyone wanted the Temple to be rebuilt. There was a leftover band of people from the former Northern Kingdom who felt displaced by the returnees. Because their capital had been Samaria, they were now called Samaritans. They never liked the Temple in Jerusalem and tried to stop the new construction. After the death of King Cyrus, construction on the Temple did stop for several years.

In the fall of the year 516 B.C.E., with the help of Nehemiah, visiting from Persia, the Temple was completed, and the Israelites celebrated their first Sukkot in the new House of God.

By the seventh month, the Israelites had settled into their homes. Everyone gathered together at the square by the Water Gate and asked Ezra the scribe to bring the scroll of the Torah of Moses, which God had given Israel. On the first day of the seventh month, Ezra the priest brought the Torah before the congregation: men, women, and anyone old enough to understand.

Ezra opened the scroll so that all the people could see. As he opened it, all the people stood up. Ezra blessed God, and all the people said, "Amen, amen." The Levites explained the Torah to the people, reading the scroll of the Torah of God and then translating it, giving the meaning so everyone would understand the reading.

NEHEMIAH 8:1–8

Under the religious leadership of Ezra and the political leadership of Nehemiah, Judaism evolved from the desert sacrificial tradition of its early years to the religion of study and worship that is familiar to us.

# Ezra's Reforms

In addition to helping Judaism evolve from a sacrificial religion to one based on worship and study, Ezra's biggest concern was keeping the Israelites Jewish. For Ezra, keeping Jews Jewish meant keeping non-Jews out!

There had always been a lot of intermarriage between the Israelites and their neighbors. Moses and King Solomon both had "foreign" wives. Sometimes these marriages brought good things to the Israelites, as in the case of Ruth. Other times it brought disaster, as with King Ahab's wife Jezebel.

Ezra determined that the way to keep foreign gods out of Judaism was to end all intermarriage. His action was strong and harsh. He declared that any marriage between a Jew and a non-Jew was hereby annulled. Every intermarried couple was suddenly divorced, whether they liked it or not. Non-Jewish wives and children were sent out of the country. The Books of **Ezra/Nehemiah** do not tell us of any protests by the people. Perhaps this is because the author either agreed with Ezra or **was** Ezra.

Ezra's attitude goes against the beliefs of the people who wrote **Ruth** and **Jonah**. Ezra's approach was isolation. The Books of **Ruth** and **Jonah** suggest that Judaism has something to give to the "nations" and that we should interact with non-Jews.

What do you think? Use the grid below to write down the advantages and disadvantages of both philosophies.

| ISOLATIONISM | UNIVERSALISM |
|---|---|
| **Preserving our ways by keeping outside influences out** | **Spreading our message to those around us and running the risk of losing our identity** |
| Advantages | Advantages |
| Disadvantages | Disadvantages |

# Daniel

The Book of **Daniel** was probably the last of all the books in the *Tanakh* to have been written. Historians guess that **Daniel** was written sometime in 164 B.C.E., even though it tells the story of a man who lived in 597 B.C.E., during the first phase of the Babylonian exile.

Daniel, the author tells us, was one of the people taken to Babylon along with King Jehoiakim. Because he was young and intelligent and came from a noble Israelite family, Daniel was forced, along with several of his friends, to study in Nebuchadnezzar's court. According to the book, King Nebuchadnezzar wanted to groom the boys for service in the royal court.

Daniel and his friends had many adventures. Because of his devotion to God, Daniel and his friends endured imprisonment, refused to eat the king's food, and even survived being thrown into a burning kiln. Daniel interpreted dreams and had visions of the future. The most famous of the stories of Daniel are the tales of the "Writing on the Wall" and "Daniel in the Lions' Den."

The "Writing on the Wall" begins at a feast. As in the story of Joseph and Pharaoh, Daniel was called on to interpret something that was bothering the king.

King Belshazzar held a great feast for his thousand nobles. He got very drunk and ordered that the gold and silver cups that his father Nebuchadnezzar had taken from the Temple at Jerusalem be used to serve the king's guests. They drank wine and praised the gods of gold and silver, bronze, iron, wood, and stone.

Just then, a human hand appeared and began to write something on the plaster of the palace wall, just across from a lamp so that the king could see the hand as it wrote. The king turned pale. He was shocked with fear. His legs turned to rubber, and his knees began to shake.

The king called for Chaldean wizards and fortune-tellers. He spoke to all the wise men of Babylon, "Whoever can read this writing and tell me what it means shall be given a purple robe and golden chains and shall rule as the third in rank in the kingdom."

All the king's wise men came, but none could read the writing or explain its meaning to the king.

DANIEL 5:1–8

When the Babylonian wizards failed to read the writing on the wall, the king called on Daniel:

Daniel was then brought before the king. The king said, "You are Daniel, one of the exiles whom my father, the king, brought from Judah. I have heard that you have the spirit of the gods in you. I have heard that you are perceptive, intelligent, and wise. The wizards and fortune-tellers could not tell me what this writing means. If you can read the writing and explain it to me, you shall be clothed in purple and wear a golden chain around your neck and rule as the third in rank in the kingdom."

Daniel answered, "You may keep your gifts. Give the presents to someone else. But I will read the writing for the king.... You, Belshazzar, were arrogant. You raised yourself above the God of Heaven. You had the vessels of God's Temple brought to you. You and your friends drank wine from them and praised gods of silver and gold, bronze and iron, wood and stone, gods that could not see, hear, or understand. But you did not praise the God who controls your breath and your actions. God made the hand appear and had the writing inscribed. This is what it says:

MENE MENE TEKEL UPARSIN

And this is what it means:

MENE—God has numbered the days of your kingdom and brought your reign to an end.

TEKEL—You have been weighed on a scale and are found wanting.

PARSIN—Your kingdom has been split, divided among the Medes and the Persians.

DANIEL 5:13–17, 22–28

That night, as the story goes, Belshazzar was killed, and the Mede (Persian) king Darius became ruler over all Babylon.

# Daniel in the Lions' Den

With the Babylonian empire gone, Daniel immediately rose in rank with the Persians. Unfortunately, some of the Persian officials didn't like the fact that a Jew was rising in rank above them. Knowing that Daniel was devoted to God, the officials devised a plot: They suggested to Darius that it be made a law that for thirty days all oaths and prayers had to call on Darius and Darius alone. Anyone who swore or prayed to any god or person other than the emperor would automatically be thrown into a lions' den. And so it became law.

But as an observant Jew, Daniel faced Jerusalem three times a day and prayed to God the traditional Hebrew prayers. Despite the new law, Daniel continued his daily prayers and was the first to be arrested for violating the law.

Darius was very fond of Daniel, and so he was saddened to learn of the violation. Nevertheless, a law was a law:

By the king's order, Daniel was brought and thrown into the lions' den. The king said to him, "Your God, whom you serve so often, will save you."

A rock was placed over the mouth of the cave and sealed with the king's signet ring in front of witnesses.

The king then went to his palace and spent the night fasting, unable to sleep. Then, at the first light of dawn, the king got up and rushed to the lions' den. Approaching the den, he cried out, "Daniel, servant of the living God, was God able to protect you from the lions?"

Then Daniel's voice came out, "Your majesty, may you live forever. God sent an angel, who shut the mouths of the lions so that they did not hurt me."

The king was overjoyed. He ordered that Daniel be brought up out of the den. When Daniel came out of the den, he had no injuries, because he had trusted in God.

DANIEL 6:17–24

The author of the Book of **Daniel** had a specific purpose in telling these heroic and miraculous stories. Let's try to determine the author's purpose.

Daniel was a Jew living in a non-Jewish world. How did the non-Jewish leaders (King Belshazzar of Babylon and King Darius of Persia) feel about Daniel?

_____

_____

What sort of thing did Daniel do to or for the non-Jewish leaders?

_____

_____

What kind of example or role model was Daniel for other Jews living in non-Jewish countries?

_____

_____

What do you think was the purpose of the author of the Book of **Daniel?**

_____

_____

*The Books of **Daniel**, **Ruth**, **Esther**, **Chronicles**, and **Ezra/Nehemiah** do not agree among themselves about what it means to be a Jew or how we should relate to our non-Jewish neighbors. Each book, in its own way, gave its early readers—and us—an understanding of being a Jew.*

# WRAPPING IT UP

The Prophets and Writings, together with the five books of the Torah, comprise the *Tanakh: Torah, N'vi-im,* and *K'tuvim.* They are the very heart of the Jewish religion. From them, we can learn about our history, our values, and our beliefs. They ask us questions and provide us answers.

In this book, we have taken a good look at the books in Prophets and Writings. What's next? We've still barely scratched the surface. Here are some of the learning places you can now go:

1. Read one or more of the Bible's books on your own.
2. Take part in a weekly Torah study at your synagogue.
3. Improve your skills with Hebrew so that you can better understand what is in the Hebrew edition of the Bible.
4. Attend synagogue services. Take note of how sections of the Bible are included in our regular worship.
5. Go to your local or school library to discover how many great books have taken names, themes, and images from the Bible.
6. Learn about Talmud and midrash. These are the many books that were written after the time of Ezra and Nehemiah—books that carry on the traditions and stories of the Bible and contain many legends and interpretations based on stories in the Bible.

In any event, before—like King Belshazzar of Babylon—you see the handwriting on the wall, take up the study of the *Tanakh.* Let it be a part of your life and your family's. Study it when you are sitting down, when you are rising up, when you are in your house, and when you are away. Keep its words on your heart, in your mind, and at your very soul.

Remembering what the Psalmist said, these words of wisdom are a Tree of Life. You will find happiness as you climb it. You will find pleasure swinging from its many branches.

Go forth, and learn.